WHAT IS A

DISCIPLE

AND HOW DO YOU MAKE ONE?

MARK SWIGER

CREATION
HOUSE

WHAT IS A DISCIPLE AND HOW DO YOU MAKE ONE? by Mark Swiger
Published by Creation House
A Charisma Media Company
600 Rinehart Road
Lake Mary, Florida 32746
www.charismamedia.com

Inside illustrations: Growing seeds page 37, Licensed by *www.dollarphotoclub.com*; Exodus map page 51, from *www.zionteacher.org*; Moses tabernacle from page 54 from *www.eltonmcmillansr.mysite.com/images/*.

Design Director: Justin Evans
Cover design by Lisa McClure

Visit the author's website: *www.markswiger.org*

Library of Congress Cataloging-in-Publication Data: 2015939482
International Standard Book Number: 978-1-62998-460-5

First edition

15 16 17 18 19 — 9 8 7 6 5 4 3 2 1
Printed in the United States of America

DEDICATION

This book is dedicated to my ministry partners, the members of the Army of 300. Together we have reached millions with the saving and healing power of Jesus Christ. Without their obedience to God, this book would not have been possible. I salute you!

CONTENTS

PART I
WHAT IS A DISCIPLE?

PART II
HOW DO YOU MAKE ONE?

PREFACE

Important information:

This manual contains both Parts I and II and is intended to be used by church pastors and leaders.

Part I deals with the subject of "What Is a Disciple?" Written in lesson format, it will help prepare the congregation to fully enlist in the disciple-making process.

Part II focuses on the details of "How Do You Make a Disciple?" It is written for those in leadership positions to implement a discipleship program.

Please make sure that you have a firm grasp of Part I before you proceed to Part II. Have all church leaders, board members, and staff work through the lessons in Part I together. This is necessary to have the consensus to go forward and to understand the changes recommended in Part II.

PART I

WHAT IS A DISCIPLE?

Lesson 1:

INTRODUCTION

I NEVER WOULD HAVE thought that addressing the question "what is a disciple and how do you make one?" would have such far-reaching implications. In seeking answers, I uncovered solutions for many of the problems the Christian Church faces today, major problems such as:

- Pastor burnout

- Follow-up and people "falling through the cracks"

- Church growth and attendance

- "Church-hopping"

- Tithes and offerings

- Immorality in the Church

- Powerless Christianity

- Reaching the lost

So, what is a disciple and how do you make one? In the two-thousand years that the Church has had to address this question, you would think the answers would have been well known by now. However, in over thirty-five years of pastoral and international evangelistic ministry, working with virtually every major denomination, I found none who had any real insight about this subject.

My journey to find these answers began supernaturally. Like most every pastor, I was not satisfied with the level of spiritual growth I was seeing in our church. Despite applying my best preaching efforts and latest programs, most people seemed to languish on the pew year after year, staying essentially the same. As far as making a difference in the world around us, the world was winning. Divorce, fornication, back-sliding, and the "cares of this world" took their toll on the congregation.

Then, in 1992, I was in my office seeking God's direction for our church. Much to my surprise, the Lord spoke and asked me a question: "Where are you taking my people?" After gathering my composure and thinking about how I should answer, I had to admit I wasn't leading them anywhere. I was just trying to keep the sheep from running away. I was in crisis management mode, putting out fires. Then, somehow, I had the inspiration to ask the Lord a question: "Where do you want me to take them?"

The Lord then showed me a vision: It was the present level of my congregation's development. How pitiful they looked. They were unequipped, unmotivated, and discouraged. They were in survival mode, barely able to stay saved themselves let alone bring salvation to those around them. When I asked them to rise up and take the city for Jesus (to bring healing, blessing, and salvation), they looked at me like I was crazy and began to complain about the struggles they faced in daily life. How could they take the city when they were just trying to keep from falling into sin themselves?

Then God showed me the same group of people, but now they had been changed. What a difference! They were "on fire," consumed with the Gospel and the cause of Christ. The cares of this world had no effect on them. They were bold and in unity. With power and confidence, they waded into the fray to take the city for Jesus. The Lord said: "That is where I want you to take my people."

At first I thought such radical transformation would be impossible. Then the Lord reminded me that in the military, they can take "mama's boys" and in a few months make mighty soldiers out of them. Is not our God able to take people and make them what He wants them to be? How could God call me to train believers to become like that and there not be a way of doing so? Thus began my journey of unlearning and learning, of discovering that God indeed has a biblical way to train His people and make them into mighty disciples.

What exactly is a disciple and how do you make one? By God's grace, I have obtained answers. I pray the Holy Spirit takes these living eternal truths and makes them part of your ministry in making true disciples. Disciples like Jesus, the Apostles and the early church made. Disciples that turned the world upside down.

LESSON 1: QUESTIONS FOR DISCUSSION

Are you satisfied with the present level of maturity in the body of believers where you serve?

Have the members of your church been properly trained and equipped to have a major influence in the community and on those around them? Are they "turning the world upside down?" (Acts 17:6).

If mature disciples are shown in the Bible to be walking in power and victory or "more than conquerors" (Romans 8:37), then what percentage of people in your church qualify? How many disciples became mature in the last year? How many in the last five, ten, or twenty years?

NOTES:

_____

_____

_____

_____

_____

_____

_____

_____

Lesson 2:

DO WE REALLY KNOW HOW TO MAKE MATURE DISCIPLES?

IT IS VERY important that we have a clear understanding of what a mature disciple is like. Why? Because we are commanded by Jesus in the Great Commission to make them.

> "Go therefore and make disciples of all the nations, baptizing them in the name of the Father and of the Son and of the Holy Spirit."
>
> —MATTHEW 28:19

We need to know exactly what it is we are making. What are the powers and capabilities of a disciple? What knowledge do they need to have? What is the function of a disciple? Just what kind of person are we producing?

The term "disciple" has become very convoluted over the centuries. If you ask one-hundred pastors this question today, chances are you will get one-hundred answers. Most of them will describe disciples something like this: "They believe in Jesus. They have been baptized in the church. They are good citizens, parents, or children. They love the Lord and each other. They are members of and support the local church and share their faith with others."

While the above description is part of being a disciple, it falls far short of the biblical definition. If leadership does not know exactly what we are making, we are building without a pattern. Without a pattern there is no rhyme or reason to what we teach, when we teach it, or to whom we teach it. This is why we go from message to message, meeting to meeting, and class to class without seeing real change in our congregations. There is no intentionality in the making of disciples, because we do not know exactly what we are making or how to make them.

For example, disciples are likened to soldiers in the Bible. Imagine you were called to make soldiers. You would need to know what a soldier was to become like. What training should he or she have? What skills do they need? How would you impart that training? After thousands of years, governments have a pretty good idea what qualities they want to produce in an individual soldier and how to create those qualities. But what if they said to the new recruits: "OK, you are in the army now. Please come for training once a week, but only if you feel like it. This week we will learn how to salute. Next week we will talk for an hour on how to make your bed. I think we may do a series next month on the 'Importance of the Gas Mask.' For you more radical and committed soldiers, we have some optional training on Wednesday nights...did I mention there will be pizza?" With this kind of approach, how long do you think it would take to make a soldier? Twenty years? Thirty years? Would they ever become soldiers?

This may seem funny, but this is exactly the approach the modern church has taken in making disciples.

Need we ask why churches are powerless? Is it any wonder that church folks stay essentially the same year after year and our communities remain lost?

Pastors have not been trained in how to make biblical disciples. Our Bible colleges taught us how to prepare sermons, preside over meetings, do counseling, give communion, do funerals, and dedicate babies. We have a mind-set that our job is to make sermons, not to make disciples.

I think we would all agree that Jesus knew what a mature disciple was and how to make one. I believe that the apostles and ministers in the first century knew how to make these powerful beings called disciples. We see it recorded in the Bible how the early disciples "turned the world upside down" for Jesus. But something happened...something the Apostle Paul warned about:

> "For I know this, that after my departing shall grievous wolves enter in among you, not sparing the flock. Also of your own selves shall men arise, speaking perverse things, to draw away disciples after them. Therefore watch, and remember, that by the space of three years I ceased not to warn every one night and day with tears."
>
> —ACTS 20:29–31, KJV

The prophecy of Paul came to pass in Church history. Men arose that did not make disciples of Jesus, but after themselves. The Church entered into a period known as the "Dark Ages." The knowledge and skill needed to make true disciples was lost. As a result pastors and leaders today have not been trained correctly in making disciples or even how to be mature disciples themselves!

I was invited by a bishop of a major denomination to teach their pastors about discipleship. After showing them in the Bible what a real disciple looks like, they had a refreshingly honest response. They said: "We are not disciples ourselves, so how can we make one?" I was blessed to be invited to return and help teach them.

LESSON 2: QUESTIONS FOR DISCUSSION

Do you see a difference in the Bible between disciples of the early Church and the disciples of today? What are some of these differences?

Do you think those serving in ministry today received the same quality of training that Jesus and the Apostles gave the early church ministers? What effect does this have on the modern church?

Why would the author call the response of the bishop and pastors "refreshingly honest"?

NOTES:

_____

_____

_____

_____

_____

Lesson 3:

RESTORATION TRUTH

To understand what God is doing today in discipleship, we need to take a step back and see where this fits in relation to church history. Restoration is a large subject in itself, but the following will serve as a brief overview.

The first century church functioned in divine order. Built upon the foundation of the Apostles and Prophets, the church grew and "turned the world upside down" with the Good News.

> "And are built upon the foundation of the apostles and prophets, Jesus Christ himself being the chief cornerstone; In whom all the building fitly framed together groweth unto an holy temple in the Lord."
>
> —Ephesians 2:20–21

> "And when they found them not, they drew Jason and certain brethren unto the rulers of the city, crying, 'These that have turned the world upside down are come hither also.'"
>
> —Acts 17:6

There was such a holiness standard in the early Church that liars fell dead (Acts 5:1–11). Visitors to the church would have their secrets revealed by prophecy and fall on their faces declaring that "God is in you" (I Cor. 14:24–25). Entire cities were filled with great joy, and miracles were commonplace (Acts 8:5–8).

The Apostles then warned that heretics and wolves would arise that would nearly destroy the church. This came to pass. False doctrine caused the church to leave biblical order and decline to the point where the world entered a one-thousand-year-long period known as the "Dark Ages." During this time virtually all biblical truth was lost. Priests purchased their office with money. Sins could be "paid off," and the church taught that you could buy your way out of hell. Worship became dead, and true preaching even more dead. Religious traditions took the place of the leading of the Holy Spirit, but God had good news for the Church!

> "Be glad then, ye children of Zion, and rejoice in the LORD your God: for he hath given you the former rain moderately, and he will cause to come down for you the rain, the former rain, and the latter rain in the first month. And the floors shall be full of wheat, and the vats shall overflow with wine and oil. And I will restore to you the years that the locust hath eaten, the cankerworm, and the caterpillar, and the palmerworm, my great army which I sent among you."
>
> —Joel 2:23–25

God promised in His Word to restore the years that were lost. He would build again the waste places and restore the lost truths. He promised that the Church of the end-time would be even greater than the first-century Church: "The glory of the latter house will be greater than the glory of the former house" (Haggai 2:6–9).

The first truth that God restored to the church was "Justification by Faith" or how to be saved. This doctrine was all but lost in the Dark Ages, but God used Martin Luther beginning in 1517 to restore this truth.

The Lutheran denomination began in this movement. The next truth was Water Baptism by Immersion. This was restored by the Anabaptists from which the Baptist denominations have their origin.

It is interesting that in history, every time a truth was restored a denomination (or several) sprang up around it. It is also valuable to observe that the previous denominations seemed to always persecute or oppose the next ones. There is a pattern that with each new truth people become entrenched around that truth. They think they have all the truth and so resist any further change.

There were other revivals such as with George Whitfield and the Wesleys in the 1700s. Their preaching of a personal saving knowledge of Jesus Christ shook England and eventually the world. From this, the Methodist denominations have their roots. Revival fires burned in Wales and spread to Azusa Street in Los Angeles. This move restored truth of the Baptism of the Holy Spirit, and the Pentecostal denominations were birthed from these revival fires.

The Bible says that in the last days *"knowledge shall be increased"* (Daniel 12:4). We have seen an explosion of teaching and truths being restored in the last one-hundred years, including teaching on the subjects of divine healing; faith; the New Wine; deliverance; prophecy; gifts of the Holy Spirit; and intercessory prayer. The Charismatic movement of the 1970s changed the worship service of virtually every church and denomination worldwide. "Speaking in tongues" has gone from being practiced by a relative few who were deemed "fanatics" to being accepted almost everywhere.

As truth continues to be restored to the Body of Christ, so will knowledge of how to bring people into Christlike maturity (making disciples). In fact, the Bible declares that all creation is longing with anticipation for God's children to be revealed in their full maturity.

> "For the earnest expectation of the creature waiteth for the manifestation of the sons of God."
>
> —ROMANS 8:19

> "Till we all come in the unity of the faith, and of the knowledge of the Son of God, unto a perfect (mature) man, unto the measure of the stature of the fulness of Christ."
>
> —EPHESIANS 4:13

LESSON 3: QUESTIONS FOR DISCUSSION

What changes have you seen take place in the Body of Christ in your lifetime? What changes have you seen take place in your local church?

Do you think God is finished building His Church? Do you think He is satisfied with the present level of maturity and Christlikeness in His people?

What further changes do you think Jesus would like to see in His people?

NOTES:

_____

_____

_____

_____

Lesson 4:

ANANIAS: A PROTOTYPE DISCIPLE

PROTOTYPE [pro′to-tīp]
Etymology: Gk, *protos,* first, *typos,* mark
The original type or form that is typical of later individuals or species.

My JOURNEY IN answering the question "What is a disciple?" began with studying the disciple Ananias about whom the Bible talks in Acts chapters 9 and 22. The Word of God does not talk about him by accident. As we study what Ananias was like and what his abilities were, we see a *mature prototypical disciple* that can be used to produce other disciples.

This is not to negate the fact that Christ Himself is the original pattern, of whom we are to grow up into His likeness in all things (Eph. 4:15). Over the years I found as I taught people about becoming Christlike, I ran into a brick wall of unbelief. (What? Me? Become like Jesus!?!) Using the account of Ananias proves these qualities can and should be obtained by believers. It also exposes the misconception that the abilities demonstrated by Ananias are only for clergy called to full-time ministry as a profession.

As we study Ananias' gifting and relationship with the Lord, we can see that he was an example of what God expects each of us to become in our day.

Let us begin by reading the scriptures concerning this first century disciple.

> And there was a certain disciple at Damascus, named Ananias; and to him said the Lord in a vision, "Ananias." And he said, "Behold, I am here, Lord."
>
> And the Lord said unto him, "Arise, and go into the street which is called Straight, and enquire in the house of Judas for one called Saul, of Tarsus: for, behold, he prayeth, And hath seen in a vision a man named Ananias coming in, and putting his hand on him, that he might receive his sight.
>
> Then Ananias answered, "Lord, I have heard by many of this man, how much evil he hath done to thy saints at Jerusalem: And here he hath authority from the chief priests to bind all that call on thy name."
>
> But the Lord said unto him, "Go thy way: for he is a chosen vessel unto me, to bear my name before the Gentiles, and kings, and the children of Israel: For I will shew him how great things he must suffer for my name's sake."
>
> And Ananias went his way, and entered into the house; and putting his hands on him said, "Brother Saul, the Lord, even Jesus, that appeared unto thee in the way as thou camest, hath sent me, that thou mightest receive thy sight, and be filled with the Holy Ghost."
>
> And immediately there fell from his eyes as it had been scales: and he received sight forthwith, and arose, and was baptized."
>
> —ACTS 9:10–18

And when I [Paul] could not see for the glory of that light, being led by the hand of them that were with me, I came into Damascus.

And one Ananias, a devout man according to the law, having a good report of all the Jews which dwelt there, came unto me, and stood, and said unto me, "Brother Saul, receive thy sight." And the same hour I looked up upon him.

And he said, "The God of our fathers hath chosen thee, that thou shouldest know his will, and see that Just One, and shouldest hear the voice of his mouth. For thou shalt be his witness unto all men of what thou hast seen and heard. And now why tarriest thou? Arise, and be baptized, and wash away thy sins, calling on the name of the Lord."

—ACTS 22:11–16

Let us now begin a detailed analysis of Ananias in Acts chapter 9 beginning at verse 10.

"And there was a certain *disciple* at Damascus named Ananias." [emphasis mine]

First we notice the Bible specifically calls Ananias a "disciple." He was not an elder, deacon or one of the "five-fold" ministers listed in the book of Ephesians. He was a disciple.

Of significance here is the Greek pronoun translated "certain" that precedes the noun disciple. "There was a *certain* disciple." This word is used many times in the New Testament. According to *Thayers Greek Lexicon*, when this word is joined to a noun, (disciple) *"it indicates that the thing with which it is connected belongs to a certain class and resembles it."* In other words, this is saying Ananias was a disciple, and he was what a disciple resembles or looks like.

It is important to note that the Lord did not send an apostle, prophet, evangelist, pastor, or teacher on this assignment to minister to Paul. He sent one of the disciples, a believer. Neither did God send Paul to a church service where ordained clergy could minister to him. God did not use any organized system or clerical order such as we have today for this work. He used a disciple.

The reason why we have those ordained to "five-fold" ministry is found in the book of Ephesians 4:11–12:

"And he gave some, apostles; and some, prophets; and some, evangelists; and some, pastors and teachers; for the perfecting of the saints, for the work of the ministry, for the edifying of the body of Christ."

Other translations clarify that the *"perfecting of the saints"* is the equipping of Christians so that they can do the *"work of the ministry."*

Here is verse 12 of Ephesians 4 in the Amplified Bible:

"His intention was the perfecting and the full equipping of the saints (His consecrated people), [that they should do] the work of ministering toward building up Christ's body (the church)."

God did not call the "five-fold" offices to do the work, but to *train and equip others* to do the work of Gospel ministry. In other words, the function of clergy is *to make disciples*. Disciples such as Ananias, who do the same ministry work as when he ministered to Paul.

LESSON 4: QUESTIONS FOR DISCUSSION

How would you rate Ananias in his ability to minister to Paul?

How many disciples do you know today who can function at this level of ministry? How many pastors?

If the purpose of clergy is to make disciples who can do this ministry, how would you rate their level of success today?

NOTES:

_____

_____

_____

_____

_____

_____

_____

_____

_____

_____

_____

_____

_____

_____

_____

_____

_____

_____

_____

_____

Lesson 5:

QUALITIES OF A DISCIPLE:
A DISCIPLE CAN HEAR CLEARLY FROM GOD

Note: Read Acts 9:10–18 again before this lesson.

THE LORD SPOKE to Ananias in a vision. We know from this that disciples can have visions. The Lord speaks to His children in many ways such as visions, in dreams, in His Word, through other people, etc. Ananias' ability to hear from God is actually a fulfillment of biblical prophecy:

> "And it shall come to pass afterward, that I will pour out my spirit upon all flesh; and your sons and your daughters shall prophesy, your old men shall dream dreams, your young men shall see visions."
>
> —JOEL 2:28

We know this was fulfilled for our day because Peter quotes this verse on the day of Pentecost:

> "And it shall come to pass in the last days, saith God, I will pour out of my Spirit upon all flesh: and your sons and your daughters shall prophesy, and your young men shall see visions, and your old men shall dream dreams."
>
> —ACTS 2:17

Even though Peter said this was a prophetic word for the "last days," some teach that God speaking to His people in these ways ceased with the death of the original twelve Apostles. This is plainly false teaching.

I had a dream when I was in my last year of Bible college. In the dream I saw a map. As I looked at the map the word "Billings" became larger and larger. The Lord said that this was the place he wanted my wife and me to go after graduation. I had never heard of Billings before, so when I got up that morning I went to the school library and looked it up in an atlas. There it was as in my dream, the city of Billings, Montana.

Because the Bible says that *"in the mouth of two or three witnesses every word shall be established"* (2 Cor. 13:1b), I asked God to also confirm the dream I had through other sources. I told no one about the dream except my wife, and we swore each other to secrecy. Over the next few months, God confirmed His word to me, once through another student and then through the faculty at the graduation service.

Not long after we moved to Billings a local pastor asked me what brought us to that city. I told Him about the dream and how the Lord spoke to me. I thought he would be happy and encouraged, but his response was: "God doesn't speak to people like that any more." I felt sorry for the pastor that he could not hear from God, but in retrospect I feel even more so for his parishioners. What kind of disciples did he make? Not only did he not teach them how to hear from God, but that they could not hear from God. Is that not the blind leading the blind?

Still I would not judge this pastor too harshly. I think he was sincere and was only repeating what he was taught by teachers he respected. The error all gets back to not knowing what a disciple is and how to make one. Because the pastor was not discipled correctly, he in turn couldn't make disciples, and so the error is passed on.

Being able to hear clearly from God like Ananias is not a rare exception, but the *birthright of every believer.* Jesus said:

> "My sheep hear my voice, and I know them, and they follow me."
>
> —JOHN 10:27

Observe the clarity of direction Ananias receives from the Lord:

> "And the Lord said unto him, Arise, and go into the street which is called Straight, and enquire in the house of Judas for one called Saul, of Tarsus: for, behold, he prayeth, And hath seen in a vision a man named Ananias coming in, and putting his hand on him, that he might receive his sight."
>
> —ACTS 9:11–12

Ananias knew the name of the street where he was to go (Straight). He knew the house and the name of its owner (Judas). He knew the name of the person who he was to pray for (Saul). He knew where the person was from (Tarsus). He knew what the person was doing at that very moment (praying). He knew that the person had received a vision. He knew that the person knew Ananias' name. He knew what to do when he arrived (lay his hands on Saul to receive his sight). He knew what was wrong with the person (he was blind). He also knew that the person was already expecting Ananias to come and pray for him.

I would say Ananias was hearing clearly about this assignment, wouldn't you? What if every disciple was able to hear from God this clearly? Bible scholars say there were 50,000 disciples just in Jerusalem at that time. What if God sent each of them on a similar mission about once a month? Do you think that would have made a difference in the community? Could this have something to do with how they "turned the world upside down?"

LESSON 5: QUESTIONS FOR DISCUSSION

Can you or have you been able to hear from God this clearly?

Do you feel you are presently equipped to minister to Saul as Ananias did?

What do you think your church would be like if it were full of mature disciples like Ananias? How do you think this would affect your community?

NOTES:

_____

_____

_____

_____

_____

Lesson 6:

QUALITIES OF A DISCIPLE:
A DISCIPLE HAS A FRIEND RELATIONSHIP WITH GOD

"And there was a certain disciple at Damascus, named Ananias; and to him said the Lord in a vision, 'Ananias.' And he said, 'Behold, I am here, Lord.'"
ACTS 9:10

NOTICE THAT THE Lord called him by his name: "Ananias." And he said, 'Behold, I am here Lord.'" Observe how there is a two-way conversation going on here. Jesus said:

"I am the good shepherd, and know my sheep, and am known of mine."

—JOHN 10:14

The mark of the mature believer is that the Lord not only knows us, but we also know Him. Ananias did not need to ask if it was the Lord speaking to him. He knew. I think this was far from the first conversation Ananias had with the Lord. The following exchange is a testimony of the nature of their relationship:

"Then Ananias answered, 'Lord, I have heard by many of this man, how much evil he hath done to thy saints at Jerusalem: And here he hath authority from the chief priests to bind all that call on thy name.' But the Lord said unto him, 'Go thy way: for he is a chosen vessel unto me, to bear my name before the Gentiles, and kings, and the children of Israel: For I will shew him how great things he must suffer for my name's sake.'"

—ACTS 9:13–16

Ananias had concerns about going to pray for Saul. Saul had authority to put him in prison. Ananias knew that Saul had been doing "much evil." The Lord did not just dismiss Ananias' feelings out of hand. Neither did He deal with Ananias as a servant and say "You heard me; I said GO!" Instead he explains the situation to Ananias as a friend would.

Jesus said in John 15:15 "Henceforth I call you not servants; for the servant knoweth not what his lord doeth: but I have called you friends; for all things that I have heard of my Father I have made known unto you."

A servant doesn't know what the master does or why he does it. A servant is told to go and he goes. In a master-servant relationship, the master doesn't explain the reasons why. A boss need not tell his employees why. If the boss tells someone to do something, they had better do it. But Jesus said, "I have not called you servants, but I have called you friends." He lets his disciples know what He is doing. Here we see Jesus explaining the situation to Ananias: "Go thy way: for he is a chosen vessel unto me, to bear my name before the Gentiles, and kings, and the children of Israel: For I will shew him how great things he must suffer for my name's sake" (Acts 9:15–16).

God is not looking to make robots out of us who must obey Him without feeling and emotion. The Bible says:

> "For we have not an high priest which cannot be touched with the feeling of our infirmities; but was in all points tempted like as we are, yet without sin."
>
> —Hebrews 4:15

One day on the mission field my wife was crying out to the Lord in prayer because of some persecution we were receiving. She prayed, "Lord, they are lying about us! They are hurting our reputation!" The response of the Lord was, "Yes, I know just how you feel." He knows what it is like to be lied about and to have His character attacked. He understood the fears that Ananias had, having faced these things Himself. He is touched by our feelings and can guide and comfort us as only a friend can. We have a "friend that sticketh closer that a brother" (Proverbs 18:24).

In the subject of making disciples, producing people who know God for themselves should be the objective. You can see this in the ministry of John the Baptist. John had many disciples that followed him. He had led a major revival and had a large ministry. As Jesus began his ministry, John's disciples left him to follow Jesus. John said:

> "He that hath the bride is the bridegroom: but the friend of the bridegroom, which standeth and heareth him, rejoiceth greatly because of the bridegroom's voice: this my joy therefore is fulfilled. He must increase, but I must decrease."
>
> —John 3:29–30

As ministers of the Gospel and "friends of the bridegroom," it should also be "our joy" to lead people into a deep relationship with the Lord. Part of making disciples is leading people into intimacy with the Lord and taking a lesser role as they mature: "He must increase and I must decrease."

LESSON 6: QUESTIONS FOR DISCUSSION

Do you feel your conversations with God are one-sided?

Would you describe your present relationship with God more as a servant or as a friend?

Does the church where you serve keep people in a position of dependency upon clergy by not leading them to full maturity?

NOTES:

_____

_____

_____

_____

Lesson 7:

QUALITIES OF A DISCIPLE:
A DISCIPLE KNOWS HOW TO "LAY HANDS"

*"And hath seen in a vision a man named Ananias coming in, and
putting his hand on him, that he might receive his sight."*
ACTS 9:12

*"And Ananias went his way, and entered into the house; and putting his hands on him said, 'Brother
Saul, the Lord, even Jesus, that appeared unto thee in the way as thou camest, hath sent me, that
thou mightest receive thy sight, and be filled with the Holy Ghost.' And immediately there fell from
his eyes as if it had been scales and he received his sight forthwith and arose and was baptized."*
ACTS 9:17–18

A DISCIPLE IS AUTHORIZED by God to lay hands on people and to pray for the sick. Ananias said: "The Lord, even Jesus, that appeared unto thee in the way as thou cameth has sent me that thou might receive thy sight and be filled with the Holy Ghost" (observe that Ananias is operating in the Word of Knowledge). So not only has this disciple been trained and equipped to heal, but also gets Paul filled with the Holy Ghost by the laying on of hands. *Disciples* can do these things. Again, I repeat that the ministry of Ananias falls under the "work of the ministry" that clergy are to train all of God's people to do (Eph. 4:11–12).

You can see confirmation to this in Mark chapter 16:

> "He that believeth and is baptized shall be saved; but he that believeth not shall be damned. And these signs shall follow them that believe; in my name shall they cast out devils; they shall speak with new tongues; they shall take up serpents; and if they drink any deadly thing, it shall not hurt them; they shall lay hands on the sick, and they shall recover."
> —MARK 16:18–20

Does Jesus say here that these signs shall follow only those that are pastors? Does He say that the supernatural shall follow only professional clergy? No. It says *"these signs shall follow believers"*: those who have been saved.

These signs have not been relegated to some other era of the Church. The signs and gifts of the Holy Spirit are not something for "showing off." We desperately need them to help people. These are tools needed to do the work of the ministry. Imagine if Ananias went to Saul and did not know about laying hands on the sick. Suppose he had been taught that only professional clergy could do those things or that the gifts were not "for his day." What if he could not operate in the Word of Knowledge or he knew nothing of how to administer the baptism of the Holy Spirit? Could God have used him to help Paul? Could God have even sent Ananias in the first place?

We will be going into this area more when we teach about "How to Make a Disciple," but how Ananias knew to use his hands in healing and to administer the baptism of the Holy Spirit is found in the Word of God.

Listed in Hebrews chapter 6 are the Doctrines or Teachings of Christ. You could say these are the subjects Jesus taught His disciples in His "Walking Bible School." One of these doctrines or subjects is called "Laying on of Hands." Being an early disciple, I can guarantee you that Ananias was taught this subject correctly. This is obvious because Ananias knew what he was doing when he ministered to Saul.

Some think that this doctrine about laying on of hands is for a select few at best, but the Bible calls this a foundational doctrine, or one of the "first principles" that should be taught to every believer.

> "For when for the time ye ought to be teachers, ye have need that one teach you again which be the first principles of the oracles of God; and are become such as have need of milk, and not of strong meat. For every one that useth milk is unskilful in the word of righteousness: for he is a babe. But strong meat belongeth to them that are of full age, even those who by reason of use have their senses exercised to discern both good and evil. Therefore leaving the principles of the doctrine of Christ, let us go on unto perfection; not laying again the foundation of repentance from dead works, and of faith toward God, of the doctrine of baptisms, and of laying on of hands, and of resurrection of the dead, and of eternal judgment."
>
> —HEBREWS 5:12–14; 6:1–2

Not only does the Bible clearly teach that every believer should function in the laying on of hands, but just plain common sense dictates this is so.

Think about it for a minute. The Bible says that "If any man have not the Spirit of Christ, he is none of his" (Roman 8:9). We know from this that all born-again believers have the Holy Spirit dwelling in them. The Bible calls Him the "Spirit of him that raised up Jesus from the dead" (Romans 8:11). So this same powerful Spirit, the One that took the dead and broken body of Jesus and raised Him to life, lives inside the body of every believer. A believer's body is called the "temple of the Holy Ghost" (I Cor. 6:19). To think that believers are powerless is ludicrous. The doctrine of the laying on of hands teaches God's people how to release the power within them to heal and bless others.

I tell people if they do not want to learn how to lay hands on people for the sake of the Gospel and the work of Christ, at least learn for the sake of yourself and your own family.

One day my wife and I heard a knock on the door and news that every parent dreads. The neighbor was there and told us "your daughter has just been hit by a car." Our youngest daughter, five-year-old Rachel, had ridden her bicycle down the street to the four-lane highway. As she was crossing it the light changed. A driver racing through the intersection was only looking up at the green light and did not see our little girl. The impact threw her all the way to the far side. My wife and I ran down the street to find her laying there. A crowd had gathered. We could hear them say "there are the parents" as we knelt beside her. I thank God we had been taught about the laying on of hands. We knew that the Healer lived inside of us. We knew how to release that power through the laying on of hands. They loaded her into the ambulance. When we arrived at the hospital they could not even find a bruise on her body.

Every believer should be taught this doctrine. We never know when we will need it. There may not be time to call for the elders or for a pastor.

LESSON 7: QUESTIONS FOR DISCUSSION

Do you feel you have been trained properly in the doctrine of the laying on of hands?

Why does every believer have power resident within their bodies?

Why do you think the doctrine of laying on of hands is listed as foundational for every believer?

NOTES:

_____

_____

_____

_____

_____

_____

_____

_____

_____

_____

_____

_____

_____

_____

_____

_____

_____

_____

Lesson 8:

QUALITIES OF A DISCIPLE:
A DISCIPLE KNOWS HOW TO
ADMINISTER WATER BAPTISM

In Acts 22, where Paul shares his experience, he says that Ananias took him out and baptized him in water. So we see it's biblical for disciples to baptize believers in water. Some people might respond: "Hey! Wait a minute here. I thought we had to wait and have a special church service. I thought you needed to be ordained clergy to baptize." Notice Saul's baptism was not like that of organized religion today. Understand what we see happening here is real church. This is church in action with disciples doing the "work of the ministry." God didn't say to Saul: "Go down to the church and present yourself to the pastor and he will pray for you to be healed. Then he will get you filled with the Holy Ghost and take you out and baptize you." God sent a disciple to do all that. Ananias said to Saul in Acts 22:16,

> "And now why tarriest thou? Arise, and be baptized, and wash away thy sins, calling on the name of the Lord."

Ananias was discipled or taught correctly about water baptism. The "Doctrine of Baptisms" is one of the foundational doctrines of Christ listed in Hebrews chapter six. Ananias understood what baptism accomplishes and its importance, and so took Saul out immediately to be baptized after his conversion. As we study the scripture we see a big difference between water baptism today and how it was done in the early church. Churches today have made a religious tradition or ceremony out of water baptism. In most churches a special service would be organized. Some are required to attend classes first. Some practice sprinkling and not biblical immersion. Some perform infant baptism.

In the Bible, we see baptism performed *as soon as possible after salvation*, such as in Acts 8:36–38:

> "And as they went on their way, they came unto a certain water: and the eunuch said, 'See, here is water; what doth hinder me to be baptized?' And Philip said, 'If thou believest with all thine heart, thou mayest.' And he answered and said, 'I believe that Jesus Christ is the Son of God.' And he commanded the chariot to stand still: and they went down both into the water, both Philip and the eunuch; and he baptized him."

Notice there was no special ceremony organized. It was not done so that a crowd could witness it. It was just Philip and the eunuch.

We again see the immediacy of water baptism in Acts 10:44–48a when the Gentiles began to be converted.

"While Peter yet spake these words, the Holy Ghost fell on all them which heard the word. And they of the circumcision which believed were astonished, as many as came with Peter, because that on the Gentiles also was poured out the gift of the Holy Ghost. For they heard them speak with tongues, and magnify God. Then answered Peter, 'Can any man forbid water, that these should not be baptized, which have received the Holy Ghost as well as we?' And he commanded them to be baptized in the name of the Lord."

We see the same truth confirmed in Acts 16:30–33 in the account of Paul and Silas and the Jailer of Philippi:

"And brought them out, and said, 'Sirs, what must I do to be saved?' And they said, 'Believe on the Lord Jesus Christ, and thou shalt be saved, and thy house.' And they spake unto him the word of the Lord, and to all that were in his house. And he took them the same hour of the night, and washed their stripes; and was baptized, he and all his, straightway."

There is a reason why people need to be baptized quickly after salvation. If you understand what happens at baptism, you will know why. You also will know why disciples should perform this and it not be limited to clergy or done in the traditions we have today.

I will not teach on the doctrine of baptisms here, but my intent is to show that there are clearly things that clergy have not been taught correctly, and so error is passed on in the making of disciples.

In Hebrews 5:12–14, we learn that when the people should have been teachers, Paul said they needed to be taught the "first principles" again. One of the first principles named in Hebrews 6:2 is the "doctrine of baptisms."

The disciple Ananias was taught correctly about baptisms and so we see him functioning in ministering to Saul in both baptisms of water and of the Holy Spirit.

LESSON 8: QUESTIONS FOR DISCUSSION

Do members of your church understand why baptism should be done as soon after conversion as possible? Are they trained and confident in administering water baptism?

Are baptisms in your church traditional and ceremonial? How could this keep someone from getting the ministry they need?

Do you think the members of the church need to be taught the first principles? Could clergy use more understanding about the doctrines of Christ listed in Hebrews 6:1–2?

NOTES:

_____

_____

_____

_____

_____

Lesson 9:

QUALITIES OF A DISCIPLE:
A DISCIPLE IS RADICALLY COMMITTED

"And one Ananias, a devout man according to the law, having a
good report of all the Jews which dwelt there."
ACTS 22:12

THE GREEK WORD that Paul uses to describe Ananias, translated in the KJV as "devout," is the word *eusebes* (yoo-seb-ace'). It is used to describe only two other people in the Bible, *both of them soldiers.*

Those two are the Centurion Cornelius in Acts 10:2 ("a devout man, and one that feared God with all his house, which gave much alms to the people, and prayed to God always") and a soldier serving under him that Cornelius had sent to bring Peter to his house in Acts 10:7 ("And when the angel which spake unto Cornelius was departed, he called two of his household servants, and a devout soldier of them that waited on him continually.").

In both cases, the soldiers were described in the context of being totally committed or devoted in their service, in that Cornelius "gave much alms and prayed to God always" and the other soldier "waited on him [Cornelius] continually."

The English word "devout" has direct connection to the word devote or devoted. This is defined as "to commit by a solemn act" (as in devoting oneself to serving God). It means to consecrate, hallow, or set apart for a purpose.

The Apostle Paul described the level of a soldier's commitment to Timothy:

> "Thou therefore endure hardness, as a good soldier of Jesus Christ. No man that warreth entangleth himself with the affairs of this life; that he may please him who hath chosen him to be a soldier."
>
> —II TIMOTHY 2:3–4

Jesus describes the level of commitment required to be His disciple in Luke 14:26–27:

> "If any man come to me, and hate not (does not love me more than) his father, and mother, and wife, and children, and brethren, and sisters, yea, and his own life also, he cannot be my disciple. And whosoever doth not bear his cross, and come after me, cannot be my disciple." [parentheses mine]

Paul described Ananias as devout or devoted *according to the law*. What is the law of God concerning devotion?

"Hear, O Israel: The Lord our God is one Lord: And thou shalt love the Lord thy God with all thine heart, and with all thy soul, and with all thy might."

—DEUTERONOMY 6:4–5

The biblical level of commitment required to be a disciple is considered very radical in our day. A person with this quality would be called a "fanatic." In contrast, the level of commitment expected of believers is very low in most United States churches today. Sunday night meetings are rare. Mid-week meetings are usually poorly attended.

How often did the disciples meet in biblical times? *Daily!*

"And they, continuing daily with one accord in the temple, and breaking bread from house to house, did eat their meat with gladness and singleness of heart, praising God, and having favour with all the people. And the Lord added to the church daily such as should be saved."

—ACTS 2:46–47 [emphasis mine]

But to solve flagging attendance, today's churches are being more "sensitive" to the people: reducing preaching to 15 minutes, shortening the worship service, having fewer meetings, and so forth. A pastor told me, "We keep all our meetings now to a 1 hour maximum." My response to that was: "That's good. One hour of flesh is better than two hours of flesh."

What did I mean by that? The pastor was correct. The answer is not more meetings or longer meetings. *Not the kind of meetings we are having anyway:* meetings that are not making any real disciples.

Jesus did not say: "Go into all the world and build buildings and listen to lectures." Neither did he say: "Go into all the world and sing songs." (This is not to minimize worship, but singing is not in the Great Commission.) What Jesus *did* say was: *"Go into all the world and make disciples…"*

LESSON 9: QUESTIONS FOR DISCUSSION

What level of commitment do you see at the church where you serve?

If people knew the purpose of church was to become a disciple like Ananias, do you think they would commit to the process?

Do the activities, programs, and meetings in your church have a goal? Are they helping create powerful and mature disciples like Ananias? How many disciples like Ananias have been produced?

NOTES:

_____

_____

_____

_____

_____

Lesson 10:

QUALITIES OF A DISCIPLE:
A DISCIPLE REACHES OUT TO OTHERS

*"And one Ananias, a devout man according to the law,
having a good report of all the Jews which dwelt there."*
ACTS 22:12 [emphasis mine]

ANANIAS HAD A good report of all the Jews that lived in the city. He was following the teaching of Christ who said:

> "Ye are the light of the world. A city that is set on a hill cannot be hid. Neither do men light a candle, and put it under a bushel, but on a candlestick; and it giveth light unto all that are in the house. Let your light so shine before men, that they may see your good works, and glorify your Father which is in heaven."
>
> —MATTHEW 5:14–16

God has created us for the purpose of doing good works that can be seen by others and so bring glory to God:

> "For we are his workmanship, created in Christ Jesus unto good works, which God hath before ordained that we should walk in them."
>
> —EPHESIANS 2:10

The Word of God admonishes that everyone should be concerned for others:

> "Look not every man on his own things, but every man also on the things of others."
>
> —PHILIPPIANS 2:4

A mature disciple of Christ has a reputation in the community of doing good works:

> "Now there was at Joppa a certain disciple named Tabitha, which by interpretation is called Dorcas: this woman was full of good works and almsdeeds which she did."
>
> —ACTS 9:36

You cannot have a good report in your community and live a life of seclusion. Some believers live a monastic lifestyle, withdrawn and afraid to move among the masses of humanity. Others consider themselves too spiritual to be bothered with reaching out to people. They say, "It is not my calling." Their focus is about their own development and relationship with the Lord, a self-centeredness.

Infants and small children are also self-centered. When a baby cries for food at 2:00 a.m., the baby is not thinking about anything or anybody else but its own needs. They do not stop to think, "I better not cry. Mom and Dad need their sleep!" But as they get older, they are expected to be considerate of someone else besides themselves. As people grow into adulthood, they should mature to the point of putting others needs ahead of their own. Parents should go hungry if needed in order to make sure that their children are fed.

It is perfectly all right for a small child or baby to be self-centered. This is normal. They are dependant upon others and unable to care for anybody else at that stage of development. In like manner, young disciples have a stage where the focus should be on their growth and development and not on others. The problem we see in the church is that most disciples are not maturing to the point of caring for others. For many, everything still revolves around themselves.

When people come to Christ they have been damaged from living in this fallen world. Wounded feelings, broken relationships, emotional and physical abuse, and other issues have twisted believers' personalities. Most are bound with areas that must be healed before we can expect them to care about others and impact those around them for Christ. Part of making a disciple is leading them to a state of freedom in order that the love of Christ can flow through them.

When people want to join the military, basic psychological tests are given to recruits. The military does not want to accept anyone who has major issues that would affect the performance of other soldiers' duties. But Christ rejects no one. He said "whosoever will, let him come," and "he who comes to Me I will in no wise cast out." In working with believers, we are making disciples from some of the most damaged and broken people in the world. There is more to making disciples than just "take these classes" or "memorize these scriptures."

We are a triune being made up of spirit, soul, and body. God has also provided emotional healing for His people. The Holy Spirit is revealed as the Comforter in scripture. Any ministry serious about making disciples will include ministry for the soul (mind, emotions etc.) in the process. We must not push people into service until they are free and whole.

LESSON 10: QUESTIONS FOR DISCUSSION

Does your church as a whole have a reputation in the community for good works? What percentage of members do?

What are some of the reasons why people do not do more good works?

Is there ministry in your church to bring people wholeness so they can reach out to others? Are they expected to do this without training or equipping?

NOTES:

_____

_____

_____

_____

Lesson 11:

QUALITIES OF A DISCIPLE:
A DISCIPLE IS PROPHETIC

Ananias prophesied to Saul:

> "And he said, The God of our fathers hath chosen thee, that thou shouldest know his will, and see that Just One, and shouldest hear the voice of his mouth. For thou shalt be his witness unto all men of what thou hast seen and heard."
>
> —Acts 22:14–15

Every disciple is to be prophetic. This is not to be confused with holding the office of a prophet or having a gift of prophecy. Christians are "new creatures" in Christ (II Cor. 5:17). Part of that new nature, together with the fact that the Spirit of God is dwelling in them, gives believers access to divine knowledge.

> "But God hath revealed them unto us by his Spirit: for the Spirit searcheth all things, yea, the deep things of God. For what man knoweth the things of a man, save the spirit of man which is in him? Even so the things of God knoweth no man, but the Spirit of God. Now we have received, not the spirit of the world, but the spirit which is of God; that we might know the things that are freely given to us of God."
>
> —I Corinthians 2:10–12

> "For who hath known the mind of the Lord, that he may instruct him? But we have the mind of Christ."
>
> —I Corinthians 2:16

Because we are part of the Body of Christ, we have the mind of Christ. Some translations put this in terms of having access to the "thoughts of Christ."

Revealing secrets is a sign to unbelievers that God is in our midst.

> "But if all prophesy, and there come in one that believeth not, or one unlearned, he is convinced of all, he is judged of all: And thus are the secrets of his heart made manifest; and so falling down on his face he will worship God, and report that God is in you of a truth."
>
> —I Corinthians 14:24–25

"We have the mind of Christ" (I Cor. 2:16b). Does Jesus know things? Then so should we.

Disciples need the mind of Christ to live a victorious life. At times there are things we need to know to avoid danger and to handle situations we find ourselves in. As priests of our family and homes, we desperately need prophetic knowledge to lead effectively.

Most importantly we need revelation knowledge to know the Lord Himself. Paul said to the church in Ephesus:

> "Cease not to give thanks for you, making mention of you in my prayers; that the God of our Lord Jesus Christ, the Father of glory, may give unto you the spirit of wisdom and revelation in the knowledge of him: The eyes of your understanding being enlightened; that ye may know what is the hope of his calling, and what the riches of the glory of his inheritance in the saints."
>
> —EPHESIANS 1:16–18

Christians are called "children of light." This is part of being a new creature in Christ Jesus. Before we were saved, the Bible called us the "children of darkness." Jesus likened that to being blind.

> "Ye are all the children of light, and the children of the day: we are not of the night, nor of darkness."
>
> —I THESSALONIANS 5:5

Most believers look at being able to know things from God as strange or unusual, but in Christ this should be the norm. It is part of being a new creation in Christ Jesus. It is part of having the mind of Christ. Moses prophesied of this day when he said:

> "And Moses said unto him, 'Enviest thou for my sake? Would God that all the Lord's people were prophets, and that the LORD would put his spirit upon them!'"
>
> —NUMBERS 11:29

> "And it shall come to pass in the last days, saith God, I will pour out of my Spirit upon all flesh: and your sons and your daughters shall prophesy, and your young men shall see visions, and your old men shall dream dreams."
>
> —ACTS 2:17

Many Bible scholars teach that Jesus' message to the seven churches is a timeline of church history. The last one, that of the church of the Laodiceans, being reflective of our day:

> "Because thou sayest, I am rich, and increased with goods, and have need of nothing; and knowest not that thou art wretched, and miserable, and poor, and blind, and naked: I counsel thee to buy of me gold tried in the fire, that thou mayest be rich; and white raiment, that thou mayest be clothed, and that the shame of thy nakedness do not appear; and anoint thine eyes with eyesalve, that thou mayest see."
>
> —REVELATION 3:17–18

The eyes of the modern Christian have not been anointed that they may see. The blind have been leading the blind, and we find most churchgoers groping in darkness along with the children of darkness.

LESSON 11: QUESTIONS FOR DISCUSSION

Do you see "having the mind of Christ" as something strange and unusual? Why is that?

Since the Bible says you are the temple of God and the Spirit of God dwells in you (I Cor. 3:16), shouldn't there be supernatural evidence of this? Talk about it.

Today, if Christians' spiritual eyes were examined, how would you rate their vision on a scale of 1 to 10, with 10 being like Ananias. Why is that?

NOTES:

Lesson 12:

THE QUALITIES ALL DISCIPLES ARE TO POSSESS

THE BIBLE CLEARLY teaches that we are "many members in one body" and that we have different functions.

> "For as we have many members in one body, and all members have not the same office: So we, being many, are one body in Christ, and every one members one of another. Having then gifts differing according to the grace that is given to us…"
>
> —ROMANS 12:4–6a

> "Now there are diversities of gifts, but the same Spirit. And there are differences of administrations, but the same Lord. And there are diversities of operations, but it is the same God which worketh all in all. But the manifestation of the Spirit is given to every man to profit withal."
>
> —I CORINTHIANS 12:4–7

The Holy Spirit has divided the gifts and gives them to every man as He so chooses. While there are clearly gifts of the Holy Spirit that are only for some, there are also qualities that *all* disciples are to have.

I liken this to being in the Army. No matter the job or area of service they will ultimately be assigned, all soldiers must complete "Basic Training." Members of our military have told me if you do not pass Basic Training, you must "go around" and take it over until you have the required knowledge and skills.

If a soldier is being trained to become a clerk typist, he may never fire a rifle in combat, but he still must learn to use a rifle before he leaves Basic Training. There may come a time when the office at the base where he serves is attacked. Even though it is not their main duty in the Army, every clerk typist will be required to take up arms. They are always first and foremost soldiers. We are always first and foremost disciples.

Here is a scriptural list of the qualities that *each and every mature disciple* is to possess:

HAS REPENTED

> "And the times of this ignorance God winked at; but now commandeth *all men every where* to repent."
>
> —ACTS 17:30

> "Nevertheless the foundation of God standeth sure, having this seal, The Lord knoweth them that are his. And, let *every one that nameth the name of Christ* depart from iniquity."
>
> —II TIMOTHY 2:19

IS BORN AGAIN

"Jesus answered and said unto him, 'Verily, verily, I say unto thee, Except a man be born again, he cannot see the kingdom of God.'"

—JOHN 3:3

"Being born again, not of corruptible seed, but of incorruptible, by the word of God, which liveth and abideth for ever."

—I PETER 1:23

IS WATER BAPTIZED

"Then Peter said unto them, 'Repent, and be baptized every one of you in the name of Jesus Christ for the remission of sins, and ye shall receive the gift of the Holy Ghost.'"

—ACTS 2:38

IS FILLED WITH THE SPIRIT

"And when they had prayed, the place was shaken where they were assembled together; and they were all filled with the Holy Ghost, and they spake the word of God with boldness."

—ACTS 4:31

HAS EVERLASTING LIFE

"And this is the will of him that sent me, that every one which seeth the Son, and believeth on him, may have everlasting life: and I will raise him up at the last day."

—JOHN 6:40

HAS RIGHTEOUSNESS

"Even the righteousness of God which is by faith of Jesus Christ unto all and upon all them that believe: for there is no difference."

—ROMANS 3:22

HAS HOLINESS

"Follow peace with *all men*, and holiness, without which no man shall see the Lord."

—HEBREWS 12:14

HAS WISDOM

"If *any of you* lack wisdom, let him ask of God, that giveth to *all* men liberally, and upbraideth not; and *it shall be given him*."

—JAMES 1:5

HAS GRACE (SUPERNATURAL ENABLEMENT)

"...and great grace was upon *them all*."

—ACTS 4:33b

"But unto *every one of us* is given grace according to the measure of the gift of Christ."

—EPHESIANS 4:7

HAS FAITH

"We are bound to thank God always *for you,* brethren, as it is meet, because that *your* faith groweth exceedingly..."

—II THESSALONIANS 1:3a

"...according as God hath dealt *to every man* the measure of faith."

—ROMANS 12:3b

HAS LOVE

"...and the charity (love) of *every one of you all* toward each other aboundeth."

—II THESSALONIANS 1:3b

"By this shall all men know that *ye are* my disciples, if *ye have* love one to another."

—JOHN 13:35

HAS PEACE

"Now the God of peace be *with you all.* Amen."

—ROMANS 15:33

HAS AN ANOINTING TO KNOW

"But *ye have* an unction from the Holy One, and *ye know* all things...But the anointing which *ye have* received of him abideth *in you,* and *ye need* not that any man *teach you:* but as the same anointing *teacheth you* of all things, and is truth, and is no lie, and even as it hath *taught you, ye shall* abide in him."

—I JOHN 2:20, 27

HEARS THE VOICE OF THE LORD

"Every *one* that is of the truth heareth my voice."

—JOHN 18:37b

"*My sheep* hear my voice, and I know them, and they follow me."

—JOHN 10:27

HAS POWER, ARMOUR, AND WEAPONS

"Finally, *my brethren*, be strong in the Lord, and in the power of his might. Put on the whole armour of God, that ye may be able to stand against the wiles of the devil."

—EPHESIANS 6:10–11

"For the weapons of our warfare are not carnal, but mighty through God to the pulling down of strongholds."

—II CORINTHIANS 10:4

"Strengthened with all might, according to his glorious power..."

—Colossians 1:11a

HAS SUPERNATURAL SIGNS

"And these signs shall follow *them that believe*; in my name shall they cast out devils; they shall speak with new tongues; they shall take up serpents; and if they drink any deadly thing, it shall not hurt them; they shall lay hands on the sick, and they shall recover."

—Mark 16:17–18

SPEAKS IN TONGUES (NOT TO BE CONFUSED WITH THE GIFT OF TONGUES)

"I would that *ye all* spake with tongues..."

—I Corinthians 14:5a

"And *they were all* filled with the Holy Ghost, and began to speak with other tongues, as the Spirit gave them utterance."

—Acts 2:4

HAS SUPERNATURAL MANIFESTATIONS

"But the manifestation of the Spirit is given *to every man* to profit withal."

—I Corinthians 12:7

"But all these worketh that one and the selfsame Spirit, *dividing to every man* severally as he will."

—I Corinthians 12:11

IS LED BY THE SPIRIT

"For as many as are led by the Spirit of God, they are the sons of God."

—Romans 8:14

HAS BOLDNESS

"According to the eternal purpose which he purposed in Christ Jesus our Lord: *In whom we have boldness* and access with confidence by the faith of him."

—Ephesians 3:11–12

IS DISCIPLINED

"For whom the Lord loveth he chasteneth, and scourgeth *every son* whom he receiveth."

—Hebrews 12:6

IS CHRISTLIKE

"Till we *all* come in the unity of the faith, and of the knowledge of the Son of God, unto a perfect man, unto the measure of the stature of the fulness of Christ."

—Ephesians 4:13

"The disciple is not above his master: but *every one* that is perfect shall be as his master."

—Luke 6:40

IS IN UNITY

"And the *multitude of them* that believed were of one heart and of one soul."

—ACTS 4:32

"That *they all* may be one; as thou, Father, art in me, and I in thee, that they also may be one in us: that the world may believe that thou hast sent me."

—JOHN 17:21

IS COMMITTED

"And he answering said, Thou shalt love the Lord thy God with all *thy* heart, and with all *thy* soul, and with all *thy* strength, and with all *thy* mind; and *thy* neighbour as *thyself*."

—LUKE 10:27

"So likewise, *whosoever* he be of you that forsaketh not all that he hath, he cannot be my disciple."

—LUKE 14:33

IS FRUITFUL

"A good tree cannot bring forth evil fruit, neither can a corrupt tree bring forth good fruit. Every tree that bringeth not forth good fruit is hewn down, and cast into the fire. Wherefore by their fruits ye shall know them."

—MATTHEW 7:18–20

"*Every* branch in me that beareth not fruit he taketh away: and *every* branch that beareth fruit, he purgeth it, that it may bring forth more fruit."

—JOHN 15:2

IS SELFLESS

"We then that are strong ought to bear the infirmities of the weak, and not to please ourselves. *Let every one of us* please his neighbour for his good to edification."

—ROMANS 15:1–2

IS A GENEROUS GIVER

"*Every man* according as he purposeth in his heart, so let him give; not grudgingly, or of necessity: for God loveth a cheerful giver."

—II CORINTHIANS 9:7

IS PRAYERFUL

"Be careful for nothing; but in every thing by prayer and supplication with thanksgiving let your requests be made known unto God."

—PHILIPPIANS 4:6

"I will therefore *that men pray every where*, lifting up holy hands, without wrath and doubting."

—I TIMOTHY 2:8

IS A WORSHIPER

"In every thing give thanks: for this is the will of God in Christ Jesus *concerning you.*"

—I THESSALONIANS 5:18

"That at the name of Jesus *every knee* should bow, of things in heaven, and things in earth, and things under the earth; And that *every tongue* should confess that Jesus Christ is Lord, to the glory of God the Father."

—PHILIPPIANS 2:10-11

LESSON 12: QUESTIONS FOR DISCUSSION

What are the similarities between the list of "disciple qualities" in this lesson and those of Ananias?

What percentage of people in the church you attend have all the attributes listed above? How many are strong in a few areas?

Could anything be done differently to help people who are weak in some areas become strong?

NOTES:

_____

_____

_____

_____

_____

_____

_____

_____

_____

_____

_____

_____

_____

_____

Lesson 13:

WHAT IS A DISCIPLE?
A POWERFUL NEW KIND OF BEING

*"Therefore if any man be in Christ, he is a new creature: old things
are passed away; behold, all things are become new."*
II Corinthians 5:17

THE THOUGHTFUL STUDY of the previous lessons provides a clear picture of what a mature disciple looks like. As we are called to make disciples it is imperative that we understand the finished product.

What becomes clear is that disciples are not "normal" in the sense that the world defines normal. Disciples are powerful beings that are "not of this world," even as Jesus said He was not of this world:

"They are not of the world, even as I am not of the world."

—John 17:16

"If ye were of the world, the world would love his own: but because ye are not of the world, but I have chosen you out of the world, therefore the world hateth you."

—John 15:19

When we become born again by the Spirit of God, we are no longer of this world. We have a new blood-line. We are new creatures. The Bible declares we are born again, not of Adam's sinful seed, but of Christ the incorruptible seed.

"Being born again, not of corruptible seed, but of incorruptible, by the word of God, which liveth and abideth for ever."

—I Peter 1:23

The Lord intends Christians to be a totally different race of beings, unlike all other peoples.

"But ye are a chosen generation, a royal priesthood, a holy nation, a peculiar people; that ye should shew forth the praises of him who hath called you out of darkness into his marvellous light."

—I Peter 2:9

The Lord expects us not to be like other people in the world, but to be transformed into His image.

"And be not conformed to this world: but be ye transformed by the renewing of your mind, that ye may prove what is that good, and acceptable, and perfect, will of God."

—Romans 12:2

Jesus did not come to earth to put a whitewash on the rotten wood of humanity. In His victorious death, burial, and resurrection, He released everything needed to transform us: Spirit, Soul, and Body.

> "Wherefore he is able also to save them to the uttermost that come unto God by him…"
>
> —HEBREWS 7:25a

> "And what is the exceeding greatness of his power to us-ward who believe, according to the working of his mighty power, which he wrought in Christ, when he raised him from the dead, and set him at his own right hand in the heavenly places."
>
> —EPHESIANS 1:19–20

> "Now unto him that is able to do exceeding abundantly above all that we ask or think, according to the power that worketh in us."
>
> —EPHESIANS 3:20

> "Even the mystery which hath been hid from ages and from generations, but now is made manifest to his saints: To whom God would make known what is the riches of the glory of this mystery among the Gentiles; which is Christ in you, the hope of glory: Whom we preach, warning every man, and teaching every man in all wisdom; that we may present every man perfect in Christ Jesus."
>
> —COLOSSIANS 1:26–28

The seed of sin that Adam planted in the human race grew until the world needed to be destroyed by flood. Man had become consumed by evil. Our heavenly Father, by use of the law and the nation of Israel, kept that evil seed from coming to full fruition again until Jesus arrived. Called the "last Adam," Jesus has introduced a new seed—an incorruptible seed—into the earth. Just as the seed of sin grew from generation to generation until mankind was consumed by evil, so shall the seed of Christ grow in the earth until a generation arises that has become Christlike. Both seeds are now active in the peoples of the earth. The Bible declares that both seeds will grow and come to fruition or maturity in the last days.

> "Let both grow together until the harvest: and in the time of harvest I will say to the reapers, Gather ye together first the tares, and bind them in bundles to burn them: but gather the wheat into my barn."
>
> —MATTHEW 13:30

> "For, behold, the darkness shall cover the earth, and gross darkness the people: but the Lord shall arise upon thee, and his glory shall be seen upon thee."
>
> —ISAIAH 60:2

The fact that a generation of Christians will arise and grow to Christlike maturity is clearly taught in the New Testament.

> "And Jesus answered them, saying, 'The hour is come, that the Son of man should be glorified. Verily, verily, I say unto you, Except a corn of wheat fall into the ground and die, it abideth alone: but if it die, it bringeth forth much fruit.'"
>
> —JOHN 12:23–24

> "Be not deceived; God is not mocked: for whatsoever a man soweth, that shall he also reap."
>
> —GALATIANS 6:7

Jesus is that "corn of wheat" that died for us. He is looking for that seed that was sown to grow and bring forth fruit after its own kind.

> "Till we all come in the unity of the faith, and of the knowledge of the Son of God, unto a perfect man, unto the measure of the stature of the fulness of Christ."
> —EPHESIANS 4:13

> "But speaking the truth in love, may grow up into him in all things, which is the head, even Christ."
> —EPHESIANS 4:15

Concerning the Second Coming of the Lord, we are admonished to have patience, because the Lord is waiting for the seed that He has sown to come to Christlike maturity.

> "Be patient therefore, brethren, unto the coming of the Lord. Behold, the husbandman waiteth for the precious fruit of the earth, and hath long patience for it, until he receive the early and latter rain."
> —JAMES 5:7

In fact all creation is waiting for this.

> "Everything God created looks forward to the time when his children will appear in their full and final glory."
> —ROMANS 8:19 (NIRV)

LESSON 13: QUESTIONS FOR DISCUSSION

What level of maturity does God expect of His people?

Jesus said He would "build His church." Is the building finished? Has His bride "made herself ready" (Rev. 19:7)?

Do people know there is a biblical way to grow and mature? If a plain path to maturity were set before them, do you think they would follow it?

NOTES:

_____

_____

_____

_____

_____

_____

_____

Lesson 14:

WHAT IS A "NORMAL" DISCIPLE?

THE SECULAR WORLD is confused about what a real Christian looks like. This is understandable, but this should not be so in the church. In many churches the requirements to be a Christian have been dumbed-down. Not only are biblical standards for being a disciple not upheld, but in some denominations the bar has been lowered to the point of accepting the sexually immoral as members and clergy. The biblical standards of morality must be evident, but along with morality a typical level of maturity must also be established.

If we are to make real disciples there is a deceitful stronghold in the minds of Christians that must be broken: *"The level of development we currently see in believers is all that God expects."*

We have seen from the previous lessons that disciples are to do the "work of the ministry."

> "And he gave some, apostles; and some, prophets; and some, evangelists; and some, pastors and teachers; for the perfecting of the saints, for the work of the ministry, for the edifying of the body of Christ."
>
> —Ephesians 4:11–12

We have seen the disciple Ananias doing this work. He helps lead Paul to salvation, heals him of blindness, lays hands on him to receive the baptism of the Holy Ghost, prophesies over him, and takes him out and baptizes him in water. A good deal of work!

Some always say to me, "That is what we hire a pastor to do!" I tell them, "We can't be hired to do your job. Our job is to train you to do your job, not do it for you. We are not hirelings."

God gave "some" pastors, "some" evangelists, "some" teachers, etc., as gifts to the Body of Christ to train them to do the work of the ministry. But we are all called to be disciples.

I explain it like this. We are all called to be soldiers, but not all soldiers are called to train others. "Some" are called to be God's drill sergeants to train and equip the disciples for the work.

Imagine if the majority of people in your church were functioning as mature disciples, serving as powerful missionaries where they work or live. I tell people they are all called to be the "pastors of where they work" or the "missionaries of their block."

To understand what your church would be like if the disciples were trained and mature:

Suppose your church was called to reach the city of Beijing, China. Three hundred missionaries were trained, equipped for the work and sent to Beijing. A "Holy Spirit" strategy was followed to reach the city. Some were assigned to reach certain geographic areas. Some were sent to work in commerce, education, government, media, and other segments of society. They formed a ministerial association to coordinate efforts. Monthly meetings for the missionaries were held for worship, to pray for each other, and to testify of the exploits they were doing. Unnecessary meetings that took time and energy away from their work were eliminated. The missionaries kept tithing to support the work. Because they were all mature disciples like Ananias, they knew the Lord's voice and were led by the Spirit. People were saved, healed, blessed, and added to the church daily. A major revival broke out and the city "turned upside down" for Jesus. The five-fold ministry worked together to make more mature disciples from the converts.

Now imagine that these three hundred missionaries were not sent to China. These disciples were trained in your local church to reach your city. How wonderful it will be when our churches are full of mature disciples!

Mature disciples should not be forced to leave family and jobs to serve the Lord. Some are called to do that, but this is not the norm. Right now we lose many of our best disciples to the "professional clergy." As soon as someone starts to function a little bit in doing the work, we "promote them" to teaching or send them off to Bible school to become a pastor. It is like taking our troops from the battle lines and sending them home to train others. Soon everyone is sitting around headquarters, reading the training manual to each other, polishing buttons, and pressing uniforms. At the same time the concentration camps are full and the enemy is sitting on the throne.

In order to change this, a great stronghold in the minds of God's people must be broken. We must reestablish the definition of a mature disciple. Until we do, many pastors will feel threatened or jealous of mature disciples, thinking they are after their job. Disciples will also continue to leave the local church to begin their own ministries, feeling it is the next step toward maturity.

LESSON 14: QUESTIONS FOR DISCUSSION

Why is it important that we break the mind-set in the Body that being called to a ministry office is the next level of promotion in a Christian's walk with the Lord?

How is being a mature disciple greater than being called to one of the five-fold gift offices?

Can someone be serving in a five-fold office and not be a mature disciple themselves? How would this affect the making of disciples?

NOTES:

_____

_____

_____

_____

_____

_____

_____

_____

_____

Lesson 15:

THE THREE STAGES OF GROWTH

ＦROM THE PREVIOUS lessons you should have a clear vision of what a mature disciple looks like. This is the end result of what we are making.

When the Lord first spoke to me about making disciples, He showed me the present spiritual condition of the church members I served and then gave me a vision of the glorious mature disciple. There was such a difference, I balked. "How is it possible to take people from where they are now to that?" I questioned. But I also reasoned that God would not call me to make disciples and there not be a way. After all, didn't Jesus take the ignorant fisherman and produce the mighty Apostles?

Like taking a journey to a far-off country, the final destination may at first seem difficult or impossible. But if the way and steps are known, the impossible becomes achievable. As the old Chinese adage says, "A journey of a thousand miles begins with a single step." When making disciples it is also like taking people on a journey. Not only must the final destination be known, but there must also be knowledge of how to get there.

The first thing to understand is the overall process. Our God is a God of order. He is called the Husbandman or Gardener. He does not just hop and skip around His garden without a plan. There is an order of growth in bringing His plants to maturity.

The Bible says we are "trees of righteousness, the planting of the LORD, that he might be glorified" (Isa. 61:3b).

Plants have 3 organs: the root, the stem, and the leaves. When a seed germinates, first the root grows down, then the stem grows up from the root, and the leaves grow from the stem. Once the plant is established, the

organs continue to grow together proportionally. Mature plants then bear fruit. Each different kind of fruit is a strategy to achieve one goal— to reproduce the plant and spread its seed.

The first key to making disciples is to understand that, just as in plants, there are 3 distinct stages of growth in the process. These stages are actually "states of being" or what we have become.

I will begin by generally describing the three stages in this lesson, and then confirm in further lessons by scripture that these stages of development are clearly God's divine order.

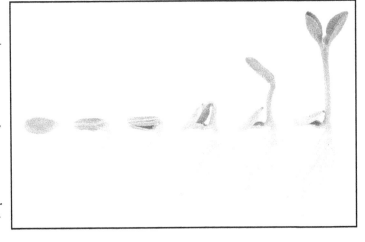

STAGE ONE: ROOT (FREE AND CLEAN)

"That Christ may dwell in your hearts by faith; that ye, *being rooted* and grounded in love."
—EPHESIANS 3:17

> "As ye have therefore received Christ Jesus the Lord, so walk ye in him: *Rooted* and built up in him, and stablished in the faith, as ye have been taught, abounding therein with thanksgiving."
>
> —COLOSSIANS 2:6–7

In the first stage we are established or "rooted" in Christ and Christ in us.

On the day of Pentecost, Peter preached the Gospel to several thousand people. Being "pricked in their hearts," the people asked Peter what they should do. Peter said there were three things that needed to be done first: 1. Repent (turn from sin); 2. Be baptized in water and; 3. Receive the gift of the Holy Ghost. Much could be said doctrinally on these subjects, but for now suffice it to say that the first stage of growth in a disciple is where they have been saved or "born again," baptized in water by immersion subsequent to salvation, and filled with the Holy Spirit (evidenced by speaking in tongues). They have turned from (been made free from) besetting sins such as: addictions, fornication, pornography, hatred, violent temper, demonic oppression or possession, etc.

The sacrifice of Christ made possible our being in Him and Him in us. As in a root system, this remains our source of life. All future growth is sustained from this. Disciples who have developed in this area are free from guilt and shame. They are not in bondage to sin and are free to serve the Lord. They have a testimony of being forgiven and "translated from darkness to light." They are new creatures in Christ Jesus. I would describe the disciple who has fully experienced this stage as being *free and clean*.

STAGE TWO: STEM (FAITHFUL MEMBER)

> "It is like a grain of mustard seed, which a man took, and cast into his garden; and it grew, and waxed a great tree; and the fowls of the air lodged in the branches of it."
>
> —LUKE 13:19

The stem, what becomes the trunk and branches of the tree, is the base that supports the leaves and fruit. If the tree grew without a strong base it would break and be destroyed. This part of the tree speaks of the stage of growth in a disciple that represents strength of character and stability. Areas such as commitment, honesty, integrity, dependability, and steadfastness. Disciples who have grown in this area are not easily blown about or moved by circumstances. They are emotionally stable. They are dependable people who are not easily offended.

God has ordained the local church be the place where these qualities are developed, practiced, and observed.

This stage of development is where a disciple who is free and clean (Stage One) commits to join a local body of believers, is in agreement with the Statement of Faith and by-laws of that body, submits to the leadership and discipline process of that church and becomes a faithful and stable person. This faithfulness is characterized by faithfulness in attendance, tithes and offerings, worship, prayer, Bible study, relationships with others, and devotional life. Disciples who have matured in this stage could be called *faithful members*.

STAGE THREE: LEAVES (FRUITFUL DISCIPLE)

> "And he shall be like a tree planted by the rivers of water, that bringeth forth his fruit in his season; his leaf also shall not wither; and whatsoever he doeth shall prosper."
>
> —PSALM 1:3

> "In the midst of the street of it, and on either side of the river, was there the tree of life, which bare twelve manner of fruits, and yielded her fruit every month: and the leaves of the tree were for the healing of the nations."
>
> —REVELATION 22:2

The third stage of growth is where disciples mature and bear fruit. This is the stage where the free and clean, faithful member is trained/empowered to lay hands on the sick, cast out devils, conduct spiritual warfare, be led by the Spirit, lead others to salvation and administer baptisms of water and the Holy Spirit. These are the basic skills that all mature disciples are to possess. A disciple who has attained this level of growth would be called a *fruitful disciple.*

FUTURE GROWTH

The three stages initially grow in this order, but then all continue to grow together *once they are established. All three stages continue to grow together proportionately, but each one must first be properly formed, healthy, vibrant, and established.*

LESSON 15: QUESTIONS FOR DISCUSSION

What would happen to a disciple if they are advanced to Stage Two without being properly developed in Stage One? What impact would this have on the church?

What would happen to a disciple if they are advanced to Stage Three without being properly developed in Stage Two? What impact would this have on the church?

What would happen to a disciple if there were no Stage Three training in their development? What impact would this have on the church?

NOTES:

_____

_____

_____

_____

_____

_____

_____

_____

_____

_____

Lesson 16:

STAGE ONE DISCIPLE:
FREE AND CLEAN

Now we will take a deeper look at the three stages of growth of a disciple. This first stage of development in the making of disciples includes repentance from sin, faith in the Blood (being spiritually reborn), baptism in water, and receiving the gift of the Holy Spirit. All this could take place in a short time as in the cases of Paul and Cornelius. The process may be spread out over weeks and months (or years) depending on what and if teaching is received.

To repeat from a previous lesson, after Peter preached the Gospel on the day of Pentecost.

> "Now when they heard this, they were pricked in their heart, and said unto Peter and to the rest of the apostles, Men and brethren, what shall we do?"
>
> —Acts 2:37

Peter then instructed them in the first steps of becoming disciples.

> "Then Peter said unto them, Repent, and be baptized every one of you in the name of Jesus Christ for the remission of sins, and ye shall receive the gift of the Holy Ghost."
>
> —Acts 2:38

STEP ONE: REPENT

Repentance is the act of turning away from sin and our own way and yielding fully to God and His way. Jesus and His sacrifice is the way that God has provided for salvation—*the only way*. Repentance must be done wholeheartedly and unreservedly. God said: "And ye shall seek me, and find me, when ye shall search for me with all your heart" (Jer. 29:13). The New Testament declares: "That if thou shalt confess with thy mouth the Lord Jesus, and shalt believe in thine heart that God hath raised him from the dead, thou shalt be saved" (Rom. 10:9). Heart belief is not just mental assent. A full repentance has a result: It is "unto life."

> "…Then hath God also to the Gentiles granted *repentance unto life*."
>
> —Acts 11:18b

When we fully turn from sin and believe with all our heart God does a great miracle. He takes away our "heart of stone" and gives us a "heart of flesh."

> "A new heart also will I give you, and a new spirit will I put within you: and I will take away the stony heart out of your flesh, and I will give you a heart of flesh."
>
> —Ezekiel 36:26

We are spiritually reborn. This is the New Covenant that God promised: "'After those days,' saith the Lord, 'I will put my law in their inward parts, and write it in their hearts; and will be their God, and they shall be my people'" (Jer. 31:33b).

Jesus said we must experience this or we cannot enter into the kingdom of God. "That which is born of the flesh is flesh; and that which is born of the Spirit is spirit. Marvel not that I said unto thee, 'Ye must be born again'" (John 3:6–7).

Repentance and the resulting new birth does a work in our spirit.

STEP TWO: WATER BAPTISM

Water Baptism by immersion subsequent to being born again is the next step in disciple-making. Some have been baptized as infants, but this does not meet the requirement of water baptism as told by Philip to the Ethiopian eunuch in Acts 8:36–37:

> "And as they went on their way, they came unto a certain water: and the eunuch said, 'See, here is water; what doth hinder me to be baptized?' And Philip said, 'If thou believest with all thine heart, thou mayest.' And he answered and said, 'I believe that Jesus Christ is the Son of God.'"

Philip ascertained that the eunuch had completed step one before permitting him to be water baptized. The eunuch "confessed with his mouth" and "believed with all his heart" (Romans 10:9). Philip knew from this that the eunuch was saved and could be baptized. An infant cannot meet these requirements.

Water baptism is not necessary for our spirits to be saved. When we die, our born-again spirits leave our body and go to be with the Lord. The thief on the cross went to be with Jesus when he died. The thief was not able to be baptized in water, but if you are going to be staying on earth and using your body you should be baptized. This is because water baptism does a work in our body. It prepares the temple of our body to be filled with the Holy Spirit. Water baptism is a physical act and does a work in the physical realm. This is why Ananias said after Paul had been born again: "And now why tarriest thou? Arise, and be baptized, and wash away thy sins, calling on the name of the Lord" (Acts 22:16). Why did Ananias say "wash away thy sins?" Was not the blood of Jesus enough to cleanse Paul from sin? Yes, Paul was saved, but water baptism does a cleansing in our body. Our body that was used by Satan to do evil works is now free to be filled with the Spirit of God to do His good works.

> "Therefore we are buried with him by baptism into death: that like as Christ was raised up from the dead by the glory of the Father, even so we also should walk in newness of life."
> —ROMANS 6:4

Take note that Ananias said to Paul concerning his being baptized—"why tarriest thou?" This is one of the many confirmations in scripture that baptism is to be performed as soon as possible after salvation. It is not right for a new creature in Christ Jesus to walk around in a body that was used by Satan. That old man is now dead, crucified with Christ, and must be buried quickly for it "stinketh." There are also legal claims that the former master has on the body. The New Testament teaches the Crossing of the Red Sea is a type of water baptism (I Cor. 10:2). If you recall, the Egyptians were chasing after the Israelites. They wanted to bring them back to Egypt to be slaves again. They owned them and had a legal claim. (We were also slaves to sin and of our father the devil.) But when the Israelites were "baptized in the sea," all the Egyptians drowned. In like manner water baptism frees us to serve God. Our bodies are "baptized into Christ's death." If a slave dies they are free from the former owner. Our bodies are then buried with Christ by baptism and raised from the dead by the glory of God. We are free to walk in a new life. Much more can be said on this subject, but let us end here with this point:

Water baptism does a work in our body.

STEP THREE: RECEIVE THE HOLY GHOST

The three steps in the first stage of discipleship—born again, water baptism and the baptism of the Holy Spirit are to be done in that order. There was one exception to this in scripture, that of Cornelius and his household in Acts chapter 10. This was a special case because the Jewish Christians at that time did not believe salvation was also for the Gentiles. When Cornelius and the others Gentiles began to speak in tongues, Peter knew they had received the baptism of the Holy Spirit. He also knew they could not have received the baptism of the Spirit unless they had been born again. Because of this Peter then "commanded them" to be immediately taken out and baptized in water. Baptism was not optional at that point because the Holy Spirit could not continue to dwell in an unholy body. So the order seen in Cornelius of baptism of the Holy Spirit followed by water baptism was possible, but an exception to the rule.

More times than I can count I have prayed for someone to receive the baptism of the Holy Spirit and felt a blockage. I would be led to ask about their water baptism experience and they had either not been baptized or baptized as infants. After receiving water baptism by immersion, they would have no problem receiving the baptism of the Holy Spirit with the evidence of speaking in other tongues.

The purpose of a disciple receiving the gift of the Holy Spirit is to receive power to become something.

> "But as many as received him, to them gave he power to become the sons of God, even to them that believe on his name."
>
> —JOHN 1:12

> "But ye shall receive power, after that the Holy Ghost is come upon you: and ye shall be witnesses unto me both in Jerusalem, and in all Judaea, and in Samaria, and unto the uttermost part of the earth."
>
> —ACTS 1:8

This is not just power to do witnessing, but to "be witnesses." Our witnessing comes from who and what we are—what we have become. The Holy Spirit is given to comfort us, to teach us, to guide us—in order to *change* us.

> "But we all, with open face beholding as in a glass the glory of the Lord, are changed into the same image from glory to glory, even as by the Spirit of the Lord."
>
> —II CORINTHIANS 3:18

> "For whom he did foreknow, he also did predestinate to be conformed to the image of his Son, that he might be the firstborn among many brethren."
>
> —ROMANS 8:29

We cannot go forward in the discipleship process and be conformed into His image without the Holy Spirit. The Holy Spirit works in us to change our soul (mind, intellect, emotions, and will) to conform us to be Christlike. This work is ongoing in the discipleship process.

The baptism of the holy spirit does a work in our soul.

IN SUMMARY

The baptism of the *Holy Spirit* does a work in our *soul*.

    Baptism in *water* does a work in our *body*.

    Repentance and Faith in the *blood* of Jesus does a work in our *spirit*.

> "For there are three that bear record in heaven, the Father, the Word (Son), and the Holy Ghost: and these three are one. And there are three that bear witness in earth, the *Spirit*, and the *water*, and the *blood*: and these three agree in one."
>
> —I John 5:7–8

PAUL DETERMINES IF DISCIPLES AT EPHESUS HAVE COMPLETED STAGE ONE

> "And it came to pass, that, while Apollos was at Corinth, Paul having passed through the upper coasts came to Ephesus: and finding certain disciples, He said unto them, 'Have ye received the Holy Ghost since ye believed?' And they said unto him, 'We have not so much as heard whether there be any Holy Ghost.' And he said unto them, 'Unto what then were ye baptized?' And they said, 'Unto John's baptism.' Then said Paul, 'John verily baptized with the baptism of repentance, saying unto the people, that they should believe on him which should come after him, that is, on Christ Jesus.' When they heard this, they were baptized in the name of the Lord Jesus. And when Paul had laid his hands upon them, the Holy Ghost came on them; and they spake with tongues, and prophesied."
>
> —Acts 19:1–6

Paul evaluated these disciples to see if they had completed the three steps of Stage One. First he asked if they had received the baptism of the Holy Ghost since they came to believe in Christ. When they said they had not even heard of the Holy Ghost, Paul then checked to see if they had been baptized in water properly. When they said they were baptized by John's baptism, (see Acts 13:24) Paul baptized them in the name of Jesus. Paul then prayed for them to receive the baptism of the Holy Ghost. The proof they received the Holy Ghost is evidenced in that they spoke in tongues. Paul made sure the three steps of Stage One were done properly and in the correct order.

LESSON 16: QUESTIONS FOR DISCUSSION

Are you spiritually born again? How do you know?

Have you been baptized in water by immersion since you were born again?

Have you received the baptism of the Holy Spirit since you were baptized in water? How do you know?

NOTES:

Lesson 17:

STAGE TWO DISCIPLE:
FAITHFUL MEMBER

Once a disciple has become free and clean, they are ready to proceed to the next stage of development. This second stage is where the disciple is matured to handle the power and authority that will be instilled in the third stage.

There is a principle that you can't exercise authority unless you first know how to come under authority. I once heard another minister give a wonderful analogy on this topic. In paraphrase:

There was a man who owned a large, successful factory. He wanted his son to inherit his business someday. A father that has any wisdom at all knows it is folly to start his son's training by giving him a position of authority. He assigned him to work in the warehouse under the strictest foreman in the place. Soon the son demanded a meeting in his father's office. "Why should I have to come to work so early?" he shouted. "Why must I obey this lowly foreman? After all, you own the factory... it will all be mine one day." The father called the foreman into the office. He said to his son: "Do you see this man? You will obey him and do exactly everything he tells you to do in every detail! You will arrive on time. You will perform your duties. Now get back to work!" The son submitted and over time advanced to become president of the company.

We also have a wise father. He requires a level of maturity before He gives responsibility. If not we will destroy ourselves and others. Pride and arrogance can have no place in the heart of a disciple. God is looking for qualities of stability, humility, dependability, steadfastness, honesty, and integrity. These qualities can be summed up in one word: faithful.

> "Moreover it is required in stewards, that a man be found faithful."
> —I Corinthians 4:2

God has ordained the local church as the place where faithfulness is instilled and proven. As we submit ourselves to the work of the Holy Spirit and the overseers set in the church for this purpose, He removes pride within us and imparts a faithful heart.

> "Likewise, ye younger, submit yourselves unto the elder. Yea, all of you be subject one to another, and be clothed with humility: for God resisteth the proud, and giveth grace to the humble. Humble yourselves therefore under the mighty hand of God, that he may exalt you in due time."
> —I Peter 5:5–6

Our faithfulness is tested and proven by measurable standards:

■ By tithes and offerings:

"If therefore ye have not been faithful in the unrighteous mammon, who will commit to your trust the true riches?"

—Luke 16:11

■ By attendance:

"Not forsaking the assembling of ourselves together, as the manner of some is; but exhorting one another: and so much the more, as ye see the day approaching."

—Hebrews 10:25

■ By submission to Church authority:

"Obey them that have the rule over you, and submit yourselves: for they watch for your souls, as they that must give account, that they may do it with joy, and not with grief: for that is unprofitable for you."

—Hebrews 13:17

■ By respect and love for other disciples:

"Be kindly affectioned one to another with brotherly love; in honour preferring one another."

—Romans 12:10

■ By prayer and worship:

"I will therefore that men pray every where, lifting up holy hands, without wrath and doubting."

—I Timothy 2:8

■ By consecration and service:

"I beseech you therefore, brethren, by the mercies of God, that ye present your bodies a living sacrifice, holy, acceptable unto God, which is your reasonable service."

—Romans 12:1

There has been some resistance by believers against the role of the local church in discipleship. Nevertheless the Word of God is clear on this subject. We must be "faithful in little" before God will allow us to advance. God has ordained the church be the proving grounds where faithful disciples are tested.

"He that is faithful in that which is least is faithful also in much: and he that is unjust in the least is unjust also in much."

—Luke 16:10

"And if ye have not been faithful in that which is another man's, who shall give you that which is your own?"

—Luke 16:12

Some resistance to church authority may stem from leaders that are guilty of "lording over the flock" (I Peter 5:3). Nevertheless, God has created the church to make disciples. This part of disciple training cannot be bypassed or obtained any other way. I have seen people who have tried to bypass this stage and the role of the local church. They always end up unstable and unable to be harnessed for the Master's use.

Being a local church member should not be confused with membership in the Body of Christ. We become part of the family of God when we are born again. For example, we become citizens of a country by birth, but if we are to serve in the army of that nation, we must enlist. We must agree to come under authority of the Army leadership and know our responsibilities. "Membership," as pertaining to discipleship, is the commitment to join a local church.

Enlisting to serve the Lord in a local church is like entering into marriage. The marriage commitment keeps people from running off when there is disagreement. Many people want to go to church without becoming official members. This is much like two people living together. They want the benefits of marriage without the commitment. People living together without being married may say they are committed, but there is nothing there to bind them to the relationship. Marriage is the commitment. Without it there is no basis for the relationship.

When joining a church, before this commitment can be entered into, there must be an agreement and understanding of the responsibilities, duties, and nature of the commitment.

"Can two walk together, except they agree?"

—Amos 3:3

There should be agreement on:

- The Church Statement of Faith, By-Laws and Church Governance

- Procedures of discipline and conflict resolution

- Level of financial support expected such as Tithes and Offerings

- Commitment to training

- Attendance requirements

- Love and support of other members

This is an important stage in the development of a disciple. It should not be entered into lightly or without proper recognition by all parties. Before people are married, comprehensive pre-marital counseling should be required. Membership classes for church must also be very comprehensive. Also, as in a wedding or an Army enlistment, an official ceremony should accompany church membership that reflects its importance. It should be entered into prayerfully and carefully.

LESSON 17: QUESTIONS FOR DISCUSSION

The Bible says to, "Obey them that have the rule over you, and submit yourselves: for they watch for your souls," telling us to submit to those in ministry over us. What would you say to a believer who has no one ruling over them or watching over their souls to submit to?

What is it like for people to become a member of your church? Do they fully understand what is expected of them? Do you think it is too easy to join? Is it easy to leave?

After people join is there any accountability to the requirements? What happens if people are not living up to the requirements of membership? How is faithfulness tracked and measured?

NOTES:

Lesson 18:

STAGE THREE DISCIPLE:
FRUITFUL

AT THIS STAGE, disciples who are free and clean and proven to be faithful are equipped to do *"the work of the ministry."*

> "His intention was the perfecting and the full equipping of the saints (His consecrated people),
> [that they should do] the work of ministering toward building up Christ's body (the church)."
> —EPHESIANS 4:12 (AMP)

Someone who is properly formed in this stage will be able to function as the disciple Ananias in ministry (Acts chapters 9 and 22). Here again are the abilities of the prototype disciple Ananias:

- Can Hear Clearly From God (Lesson 5)

- Has a Friend Relationship With God (Lesson 6)

- Knows How to Lay Hands (Lesson 7)

- Knows How to Administer Water Baptism (Lesson 8)

- Reaches Out to Others (Lesson 9)

- Is Radically Committed (Lesson 10)

- Is Prophetic (Lesson 11)

Disciples who have matured in this stage will be confident in:

- Their close relationship with the Lord

- Knowing God's voice and leading of the Spirit leading others to Christ

- Baptisms

- Healing the sick

- Casting out devils

■ Spiritual warfare

Repeat from lesson 16: *All three stages continue to grow together proportionately, but each one must first be properly formed, healthy, vibrant, and established.*

REVIEW LESSON 12:
THE QUALITIES EVERY MATURE DISCIPLE IS TO POSSESS

■ Has repented

■ Is born again

■ Is water baptized

■ Is filled with the Spirit

■ Has grace (supernatural enablement)

■ Has faith

■ Has love

■ Has peace

■ Has an anointing to know

■ Hears the voice of the Lord

■ Has power, armour, and weapons

■ Has supernatural signs

■ Speaks in tongues (not to be confused with the gift of tongues)

■ Has supernatural manifestations

■ Is led by the Spirit

■ Has boldness

■ Is disciplined

■ Is christlike

■ Is in unity

■ Is committed

■ Is fruitful

- Is selfless

- Is a generous giver

- Is prayerful

- Is a worshiper

THE ATTITUDE OF THE DISCIPLE
GOING FORWARD FROM STAGE THREE:

"Not as though I had already attained, either were already perfect: but I follow after, if that I may apprehend that for which also I am apprehended of Christ Jesus. Brethren, I count not myself to have apprehended: but this one thing I do, forgetting those things which are behind, and reaching forth unto those things which are before, I press toward the mark for the prize of the high calling of God in Christ Jesus. Let us therefore, as many as be perfect, be thus minded: and if in any thing ye be otherwise minded, God shall reveal even this unto you. Nevertheless, whereto we have already attained, let us walk by the same rule, let us mind the same thing."

—PHILIPPIANS 3:12–16

Those who have attained to the level of functioning in the work of disciple ministry should not feel they have arrived, but press on to grow in Christ and the knowledge of Him. They should continue to walk in unity along with other disciples functioning at the level they have already attained. They should remain Free and Clean, Faithful and Fruitful disciples.

LESSON 18: QUESTIONS FOR DISCUSSION

What would your church be like if the majority of people were functioning as mature disciples?

What impact could this have on your community?

NOTES:

_____

_____

_____

_____

_____

_____

_____

Lesson 19:

THE THREE STAGES IN THE JOURNEY OF THE CHILDREN OF ISRAEL

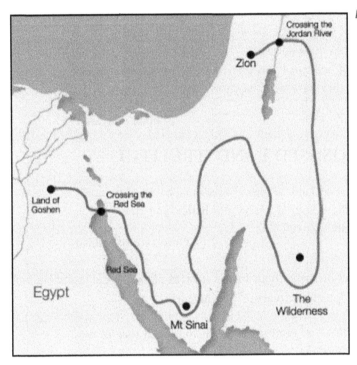

THE FIRST DISCIPLES did not yet have the benefit of the New Testament scriptures. The discipleship growth process was taught through the Old Testament types and shadows. They still help us understand disciple-making today. A volume could be written on each of these types to fully develop them, but a quick overview of each will show the three stages as the biblical pattern of discipleship.

STAGE ONE: OUT OF EGYPT (FREE)

The journey of the children of Israel began when they were in bondage as slaves in Egypt. Pharaoh, a type of Satan, would not let the people go free. God raised up Moses, a type of Christ, to lead the people out of slavery. Even though God did mighty signs and wonders through Moses, Pharaoh would not let the people go. Only when the blood of the firstborn was shed, and the children of God saved from death by the blood of the Passover Lamb, did Pharaoh release the people. The New Testament teaches that this was a type of how the sacrifice of Christ set us free from the power of Satan. Jesus Christ was crucified on the observance of that very same Passover day. We were translated out of the kingdom of darkness (Egypt) into God's kingdom or rule. We are no longer slaves to sin. This coincides with being born again: the first step of discipleship. The first stage of their journey continued with the crossing of the Red Sea and experiencing the manifest presence of God in the cloud. The New Testament reveals that these were types of Water Baptism and the Baptism of the Holy Spirit:

> "Moreover, brethren, I would not that ye should be ignorant, how that all our fathers were under the cloud, and all passed through the sea; And were all baptized unto Moses in the cloud and in the sea."
>
> —I CORINTHIANS 10:1–2

STAGE TWO: THE WILDERNESS (FAITHFUL)

In this stage of the journey, God proved the people to see if they had the qualities of faithfulness necessary to go forward into the Promised Land. It was God's intention to bring them all into their inheritance, but that generation died without entering into what God had promised them. Rebellion against God and His leadership, unbelief, being stiff-necked, pride, and other issues kept them from completing their journey. Of those people, only Joshua and Caleb, who the Bible says "wholly followed the Lord," were allowed to proceed to the next stage of the journey and possess the land. The Israelites' experience in the wilderness teach about the faithful qualities disciples must have before coming into a place of fruitful victory. Today, God has ordained that the local church instill and prove these qualities. The New Testament confirms this stage of discipleship is valid for us today:

> "Wherefore (as the Holy Ghost saith, Today if ye will hear his voice, Harden not your hearts, as in the provocation, in the day of temptation in the wilderness: When your fathers tempted me, proved me, and saw my works forty years. Wherefore I was grieved with that generation, and said, They do alway err in their heart; and they have not known my ways. So I sware in my wrath, They shall not enter into my rest.)"
>
> —Hebrews 3:7–11

STAGE THREE: THE PROMISED LAND (FRUITFUL)

> "For the Lord thy God bringeth thee into a good land, a land of brooks of water, of fountains and depths that spring out of valleys and hills; a land of wheat, and barley, and vines, and fig trees, and pomegranates; a land of oil olive, and honey."
>
> —Deuteronomy 8:7–8

The last stage of the journey of the Children of Israel brought them into a fruitful place. God's intention was to set them forth as a blessed people: A peculiar or "precious treasure" in the earth.

> "For thou art a holy people unto the Lord thy God, and the Lord hath chosen thee to be a *peculiar people* unto himself, above all the nations that are upon the earth."
>
> —Deuteronomy 14:2

The New Testament teaches that God's desire to have this nation of people in the earth is now fulfilled in those who have become the people of God through Jesus Christ.

> "But ye are a chosen generation, a royal priesthood, a holy nation, a peculiar people; that ye should shew forth the praises of him who hath called you out of darkness into his marvellous light; which in time past were not a people, but are now the people of God: which had not obtained mercy, but now have obtained mercy."
>
> —I Peter 2:9–10

God's purpose for this "peculiar people" has not changed. We are to come into a fruitful place of doing His good works.

> "Who gave himself for us, that he might redeem us from all iniquity, and purify unto himself a *peculiar people*, zealous of good works."
>
> —Titus 2:14

LESSON 19: QUESTIONS FOR DISCUSSION

Talk about the Old Testament type of a Stage One disciple (Coming out of Egypt) and compare this to your journey as a follower of Christ.

Discuss the Old Testament type of a Stage Two disciple (The Wilderness) and relate this to your journey as a follower of Christ.

Compare the Old Testament type of a Stage Three disciple (The Promised Land) and your experience as a follower of Christ.

NOTES:

Lesson 20:

THE THREE STAGES IN THE TABERNACLE OF MOSES

WHEN JESUS DIED on the cross, the veil that hid the room in the temple called the "Holy of Holies" was torn. The Bible says this signified that a way had been made for us to enter into that place. Before this, only once each year could the Jewish high priest enter there with a blood offering for his sins and the sins of the people. Now by the precious blood of Jesus we can have access to the Holy of Holies. But while the veil has been torn, there still remains a straight and narrow way to enter that place. There are other areas in the tabernacle that one must pass through on the way in: The Outer Court, Holy Place and then the Holy of Holies.

STAGE ONE: OUTER COURT

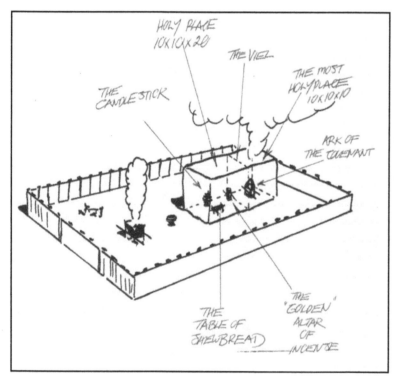

The first thing encountered when entering the outer court of the tabernacle was the Brazen Altar. This is where the blood sacrifices were made. This is a type of the Cross of Jesus where our sins are forgiven and we are Born Again. The next thing encountered on the way was the Laver. The priests had to wash themselves in this before they could proceed. This speaks of Water Baptism. Also in the outer court, covering the tent containing the Holy Place and the Holy of Holies, was a cloud of God's Glory. This was a type of the Holy Spirit. These things coincide with the journey of the Christian disciple. First being born again, baptized in water and baptized in the Holy Spirit. These prepare us to go forward and are also the things Peter told the new believers to do in the book of Acts:

"Then Peter said unto them, 'Repent, and be baptized every one of you in the name of Jesus Christ for the remission of sins, and ye shall receive the gift of the Holy Ghost.'"

—ACTS 2:38

STAGE TWO: HOLY PLACE

There were three pieces of furniture in this room that stood before the veil and the Holy of Holies: The Lampstand, Table of Shewbread, and the Altar of Incense. The Holy Place was a place of faithful service unto the Lord. The lamps in the Lampstand could not be allowed to go out. The oil had to be replenished and the wicks trimmed daily. The Table of Shewbread required that fresh bread constantly be prepared. Incense had to be prepared and offered at certain times. These things speak of a disciple's faithfulness in worship, giving, prayer, devotional life and service in the House of the Lord. All of these things needed to be done exactly as the Lord instructed. This took obedience and consecration. The Lord was looking for wholehearted dedication and a spirit of excellence.

> "His lord said unto him, 'Well done, thou good and faithful servant: thou hast been faithful over a few things, I will make thee ruler over many things: enter thou into the joy of thy lord.'"
>
> —MATTHEW 25:21

STAGE THREE: HOLY OF HOLIES

> "And there I will meet with thee, and I will commune with thee from above the mercy seat, from between the two cherubims which are upon the ark of the testimony."
>
> —EXODUS 25:22a

The Holy of Holies within the veil contained the Ark of the Covenant. Above the Ark was the Mercy Seat. God Himself communed with Moses there. No one else was permitted to go there except the High Priest and that was only once per year under very strict guidelines. To think we now have access into this place of intimate communion with God by the blood of Jesus is too wonderful to comprehend.

As we mature and commune with the Lord we see His love and concern for people. If anyone tells you they love the Lord but they show no love for others or have no concern for their souls, you know they do not know Him. The fruit of our knowing God is manifest by our love for others.

> "Beloved, let us love one another: for love is of God; and every one that loveth is born of God, and knoweth God. He that loveth not knoweth not God; for God is love."
>
> —I JOHN 4:7–8

This is also borne out by the Words of our Lord Jesus:

> "Jesus said unto him, 'Thou shalt love the Lord thy God with all thy heart, and with all thy soul, and with all thy mind. This is the first and great commandment. And the second is like unto it, Thou shalt love thy neighbour as thyself. On these two commandments hang all the law and the prophets.'"
>
> —MATTHEW 22:37–40

The fruit of a mature disciple will manifest in love for God, others and in good works. We do not do these good works to earn a relationship with God, rather these works come forth from our relationship.

The New Testament confirms the Tabernacle is a map for the journey of a disciple:

> "Having therefore, brethren, boldness to enter into the holiest by the blood of Jesus, By a new and living way, which he hath consecrated for us, through the veil, that is to say, his flesh; And having an high priest over the house of God;

"Let us draw near with a true heart in full assurance of faith, having our hearts sprinkled from an evil conscience, and our bodies washed with pure water. (Stage One—Free And Clean)

"Let us hold fast the profession of our faith without wavering; (for he is faithful that promised;) (Stage Two—Faithful)

"And let us consider one another to provoke unto love and to good works:" (Stage Three—Fruitful)

—HEBREWS 10:19–24

[parenthetical 'stage' notes mine]

IN SUMMARY

The last two lessons are brief examples of how New Testament discipleship was foreshadowed in the Old Testament. There are other Old Testament types that contain the three stages of growth. (For example, research the journey of Elijah and his disciple Elisha as they traveled from Gilgal to Bethel to Jericho. Study the three names of these places and you will see the three stages of discipleship.)

LESSON 20: QUESTIONS FOR DISCUSSION

Talk about the Old Testament type of a Stage One disciple depicted by the Outer Court and compare this to your journey as a follower of Christ.

Discuss the Old Testament type of a Stage Two disciple reflected by the Holy Place and relate this to your journey as a follower of Christ.

Compare the Old Testament type of a Stage Three disciple as seen in the Holy of Holies and your experience as a follower of Christ.

NOTES:

_____

_____

_____

_____

_____

_____

_____

Lesson 21:

THE THREE STAGES
IN THE NEW TESTAMENT

IN THE PARABLE OF THE SOWER

In Jesus' parable of the sower (Matthew 13, Mark 4, Luke 8), the reasons why people do not mature at each stage are revealed:

> "Now the parable is this: The seed is the word of God. Those by the way side are they that hear; then cometh the devil, and taketh away the word out of their hearts, lest they should believe and be saved. They on the rock are they, which, when they hear, receive the word with joy; and these have no root, which for a while believe, and in time of temptation fall away. And that which fell among thorns are they, which, when they have heard, go forth, and are choked with cares and riches and pleasures of this life, and bring no fruit to perfection. But that on the good ground are they, which in an honest and good heart, having heard the word, keep it, and bring forth fruit with patience."
>
> —Luke 8:11–15

The first group is the people who hear the Gospel and do not believe. These are the lost or unsaved.

The next group is people who fail in Stage One. They believe for a time but because they have no root fall away. How often we see people who accept Christ with gladness, but fail to be rooted in Him. They do not develop in Stage One and are not established in the faith. They never become truly free and clean. When temptation or persecution comes they fall away or backslide.

Next we see a group that has grown to Stage Two but do not mature to the point of bearing fruit. This is because as they developed, the thorns absorbed the energy needed to produce fruit. They were choked. Jesus said the thorns represent the "cares and riches and pleasures of this life." How often we see Christians never mature to fruition because their time, treasure and talents are diverted into the things of the world. They never become faithful in the things of God.

"But that on the good ground are they, which in an honest and good heart, having heard the word, keep it, and bring forth fruit with patience." Jesus reveals why these Stage Three believers are fruitful. They are not just "hearers of the word but doers" (James 1:22). They keep the word. The word "patience" used here has reference in that "we shall reap if we faint not" (Gal. 6:9). There is the quality of an overcomer in one that perseveres to fruit-bearing maturity.

AS MENTIONED BY THE APOSTLE JOHN

> "I write unto you, little children, because your sins are forgiven you for his name's sake. I write unto you, fathers, because ye have known him that is from the beginning. I write unto you,

young men, because ye have overcome the wicked one. I write unto you, little children, because ye have known the Father. I have written unto you, fathers, because ye have known him that is from the beginning. I have written unto you, young men, because ye are strong, and the word of God abideth in you, and ye have overcome the wicked one."

—I JOHN 2:12–14

Three distinct stages of growth are mentioned here and repeated: Little children, young men, and fathers. The fact they are repeated tells us these distinctions are established by God.

"… In the mouth of two or three witnesses shall every word be established."

—II CORINTHIANS 13:1b

IN THE LIFE OF THE APOSTLE PAUL

In Paul's life the three stages of discipleship can clearly be seen.

STAGE ONE: After meeting Christ on the road to Damascus, Saul (Paul) was born again, baptized in water, and filled with the Holy Spirit. He testified in the Damascus synagogues that Jesus is the Son of God and the Jews in Damascus tried to kill him, so the disciples sent him to Jerusalem. In Jerusalem, the Grecians also "went about to slay him." I see Saul in this stage as zealous but without wisdom. Because Saul caused unrest everywhere, the brethren in Jerusalem sent him to his birthplace in Tarsus. After Saul was sent to Tarsus, the very next verse says:

"Then had the churches rest throughout all Judaea and Galilee and Samaria, and were edified; and walking in the fear of the Lord, and in the comfort of the Holy Ghost, were multiplied."

—ACTS 9:31

STAGE TWO: Paul then spent several years in Tarsus. The Scriptures are almost silent concerning this time in his life, but we know that he was there in the local church anywhere from 4 to 10 years. Perhaps he was making tents as was his trade. In submission to the church leaders in Tarsus, God could deal with Saul's pride, self-will, and ambition that caused the churches unrest in Damascus and Jerusalem.

STAGE THREE: Antioch: When God saw Saul had developed qualities of stability and faithfulness, He sent Barnabas to Tarsus to find Saul. Barnabas had been sent by the church at Jerusalem to Antioch, and he took Saul with him to assist in the work there. After they spent a year teaching in Antioch, the saints at Antioch took up a collection for the church in Jerusalem and sent Barnabas and Saul to deliver the gift. Antioch was a stage in Saul's training where he grew in doing the work of the ministry. After they returned to Antioch they were ministering there for some time when:

"As they ministered to the Lord, and fasted, the Holy Ghost said, 'Separate me Barnabas and Saul for the work whereunto I have called them.'"

—ACTS 13:2

Because Saul was called to the office of apostle, he was separated from the local church at Antioch for this work. (Note: Not all Stage Three fruitful disciples are called to a five-fold ministry office and separated from the local church.) Also we see in scripture Saul is now called by his name Paul from this stage forward. A sign of his changed nature and personality.

IN THE EARTHLY DISCIPLES OF JESUS

Jesus did not relate to all His disciples in the same way. Training and teaching differed between groups that were obviously at different stages of development.

■ We see a group of believers that Jesus did not commit Himself to for training.

"Now when he was in Jerusalem at the passover, in the feast day, many believed in his name, when they saw the miracles which he did. But Jesus did not commit himself unto them, because he knew all men, And needed not that any should testify of man: for he knew what was in man."
—JOHN 2:23–25

■ We see a group of 70 disciples that Jesus had invested Himself into:

"After these things the Lord appointed other seventy also, and sent them two and two before his face into every city and place, whither he himself would come."
—LUKE 10:1

■ There was a group of 12 disciples that Jesus selected for training as apostles:

"And when it was day, he called unto him his disciples: and of them he chose twelve, whom also he named apostles."
—LUKE 6:13

■ From these twelve, there was a group of three that were given even more intimate access to Jesus:

"And he suffered no man to follow him, save Peter, and James, and John the brother of James."
—MARK 5:37

"And it came to pass about an eight days after these sayings, he took Peter and John and James, and went up into a mountain to pray."
—LUKE 9:28

As we study Christ in His making of disciples, it is clear they were not all taught the same things at the same time. They were divided according to how the Lord discerned their present spiritual state and commitment.

IN THE DISCIPLES WHO INCREASED
THEIR TALENTS (BORE FRUIT)

"His lord said unto him, 'Well done, thou *good* (Stage One) and *faithful* (Stage Two) *servant*: (Stage Three) thou hast been faithful over a few things, I will make thee ruler over many things: enter thou into the joy of thy lord.'"
—MATTHEW 25:21
[emphasis and parenthesis mine]

LESSON 21: QUESTIONS FOR DISCUSSION

Can you think of people in your church that are "stuck" in one of the three stages? Can anything be done to help them?

Did Jesus allow everyone to attend all His training classes? Do we allow everyone? Why could this be a problem?

If people knew there were three stages to becoming a mature disciple, do you think more would sign up for the journey?

NOTES:

_____

_____

_____

_____

_____

_____

_____

_____

_____

_____

_____

_____

_____

_____

_____

_____

_____

Lesson 22:

ARE YOU READY FOR CHANGE?

AFTER WALKING WITH the Lord for over 40 years, I eventually reached a certain level of maturity as a disciple. I was blessed to sit under some of the most anointed ministers of our day, yet it took me decades to get to my present state.

I developed to the place I am now like everyone else has: the work of the Holy Spirit, teaching by various men and women of God, Bible schools and colleges, books, Sunday schools, small groups, conferences, Christian media, personal study, prayer, devotional life, fellowship, impartation, life's experiences, etc. While God has used all these things, I now realize I would have gotten so much farther, much faster, if my discipleship training had been done in a biblical and intentional way.

As I studied the disciple Ananias, I saw that most pastors now serving in ministry are not able to function at that level. Some leaders today would give Ananias the title of apostle because of his abilities. If living in our time he would be appointed pastor of a large church or the head of some great ministry. But in his day, Ananias was one of the multitudes of disciples who helped turn the world upside down.

How did Jesus, the apostles, and the early church leaders create these powerful beings called disciples? It did not take them decades to make a disciple. There must have been a way. There are lost disciple-making secrets yet to be restored.

To go forward we must be brutally honest with ourselves and others.

> "Because thou sayest, I am rich, and increased with goods, and have need of nothing; and knowest not that thou art wretched, and miserable, and poor, and blind, and naked: I counsel thee to buy of me gold tried in the fire, that thou mayest be rich; and white raiment, that thou mayest be clothed, and that the shame of thy nakedness do not appear; and anoint thine eyes with eyesalve, that thou mayest see. As many as I love, I rebuke and chasten: be zealous therefore, and repent."
> —REVELATION 3:17–19

As pastors and leaders, it is very humbling to admit we "knowest not." We are supposed to know. People expect us to know.

As a young man, I started to show some skill where I worked. I will never forget what a co-worker said to me: "In the land of the blind, the one-eyed man is king." As far as our discipleship making skills go, that pretty much sums up the state of things in the Body of Christ today.

> "For I say, through the grace given unto me, to every man that is among you, not to think of himself more highly than he ought to think; but to think soberly, according as God hath dealt to every man the measure of faith."
> —ROMANS 12:3

Much about making disciples is not only about learning how, but un-learning. It took years for my eyes to be opened and see the changes that need to be made if we are going to make mature disciples.

In the final analysis, this is all really about *change*. If we are going to see disciples made, there are many changes that must happen. This is going to affect almost everything we do in our churches because almost everything we do in church is not helping to make disciples!

Making disciples will most likely change:

- Membership Requirements

- Sunday School

- Church Government

- Small Groups

- Training Methods

- Teaching and Preaching

- Accountability

- Baptisms

- Church Discipline

- Use of the Gifts

- Five-Fold Ministry

- Finances

- Order of Services

- Relationships Between Mature Disciples and Clergy

- Youth Programs

Many people have been praying for revival...revival in our churches...revival in the nations. Revivals are always about change. If you have been praying for revival, you have really been praying for change. You see, God is holding nothing back from us. The Bible says: "He that spared not his own Son, but delivered him up for us all, how shall he not with him also freely give us all things?" (Romans 8:32). God wants revival more than we do. If we were doing things His way, we would be in revival. But our eyes need to be open to see the changes He wants us to make, and our hearts must be willing to make those changes.

For the last 30 years or so in America, there has been a movement to get people to pray for revival. The main Scripture driving the initiative has been:

"If my people, which are called by my name, shall humble themselves, and pray, and seek my face, and turn from their wicked ways; then will I hear from heaven, and will forgive their sin, and will heal their land."

—II Chronicles 7:14

As can be seen in the above scripture, prayer is only one of the requirements. The others are humility, seeking God's face, and turning from wickedness. In the subject of making disciples, first we must be humble enough to admit that we do not know much of anything. (For those among us that think themselves experts in discipleship, tell me how many Ananiases your church or denomination has produced in the last 5 years? In the last 50 years? 100 years? How is that working for you? Is your church "turning the world upside down," or is your church becoming more like the world?)

Next we must pray and seek God's face. The face is where we communicate by speech and show our feelings through expressions. When we seek God's face, we are asking: "How do you feel about this Lord? What are You saying about this matter?"

We then must turn from our wicked ways. Wickedness is not just the overt sins we commit. It is the things we do that are not of God—dead religious works that have no life in them. Is it not wickedness to keep the people of God bound in systems that are unable or unwilling to make them into disciples? Isn't it wrong to take the money, time, and energy of God's people and consume it without producing any disciples? What is righteous about keeping believers trapped in a perpetual state of immaturity, not allowing them to grow, and hindering those who would? (If someone shows any potential to be a disciple, we send them away to seminaries and colleges which in turn produce ministers unable to make disciples.) Isn't it evil to be slaves to pointless religious activity and not obey the great commission of Christ to "make disciples"?

LESSON 22: QUESTIONS FOR DISCUSSION

Are you tired of church services and meetings? Are you feeling worn out or burned out?

Do you think there could be more effective methods to making mature disciples than what you are using?

Are you open and willing to make radical changes if they are biblical?

NOTES:

_____

_____

_____

_____

_____

_____

PART II

HOW DO YOU MAKE ONE?

INTRODUCTION

FOR THE PAST decade, I have traveled in the United States, Germany, and Paraguay meeting with pastors about discipleship. At times I temporarily relocated, working with some pastors for months at a time. This, combined with my own pastoral experience serving three churches in the United States over a 15-year period and then heading an international evangelistic ministry for over ten years, helped to produce this manual.

The Lord led me to experience a wide variety of church denominations, systems of church governance, and pastoral management styles. I saw first-hand what works, what does not work, and why. Coupled with prayerful study, I believe this material will serve as a tool to help churches initiate real discipleship.

I understand some people will reject the notion that these glorious beings the Bible calls disciples can be made. They will not enter in for the same reason given that the generation of Israelites that died in the wilderness failed to enter the Promised Land: Unbelief (Hebrews 3:19). This is because:

1. They have not obtained this level of maturity themselves. (They have not experienced the Promised Land; therefore it does not exist.)

2. They do not believe that God is able bring Christians into this level maturity. (The "giants" in people are too great to overcome.)

3. They fear the changes needed to go forward and prefer the "safety" of the known. (It is better to stay in the wilderness of existing structures and traditions than enter a new land.)

On the other hand, I know there are multitudes of "Joshuas and Calebs" in this generation. I have met many of them. God has been raising them up to boldly lead His people. They will possess all that Jesus died for them to have. To them I quote:

> "Be strong and of a good courage: for unto this people shalt thou divide for an inheritance the land, which I sware unto their fathers to give them."
> —JOSHUA 1:6

Can you hear what the Spirit is saying to the church?

DISCIPLESHIP PROGRAM OVERVIEW

I̲T̲ I̲S̲ N̲O̲T̲ enough to know what the people are to become like. There must be a plan to develop them. To be successful, the plan must have the following elements:

- Be clear with identifiable and obtainable levels of growth and maturity.

- Be able to take the newest babe to full maturity.

- Be flexible so that those who have already obtained a certain level can be "grandfathered."

- Be manageable.

- Be biblical.

Here in Part II, "How Do You Make One?" is a plan that includes these elements, presented along with instructions of how to implement the plan. This has been broken down into six steps, with instructions and recommendations under each step.

SIX STEPS TO BECOMING A DISCIPLE-MAKING CHURCH

1. Impart the Vision.

2. Recruit/Enlist Disciples.

3. Evaluate the Recruits.

4. Train the Disciples.

5. Practice Accountability and Discipline.

6. Provide Recognition and Support.

Each of these 6 steps is critical to successful disciple-making. They should be taken thoughtfully and prayerfully. Adequate time and energy must be allocated in each phase.

Step One:

IMPART THE VISION

IMPARTING VISION TO LEADERSHIP

For discipleship to work, the vision must first be imparted into the minds and hearts of the leadership. If the pastors, staff, and elders do not have real ownership, discipleship will end up being just a façade.

I must be brutally honest here. Having been a pastor for many years and working with them, I understand we are primarily trained as "meeting-makers" and not disciple-makers. Because of this, pastors are always looking for new material to prepare messages. When I have presented discipleship concepts in the past, some pastors saw value in them to do another series of meetings (e.g. preaching a few weeks on prayer, a few weeks on family life, and a few weeks on discipleship, etc.). If discipleship is approached on this basis, it is better not to address it at all.

Discipleship is not doing a series of messages to fill time and earn a salary. Discipleship is a *commission*. We have been commanded by Jesus Christ Himself to perform the duty of making disciples. We have been given authority by Jesus to act in His behalf to accomplish this mission. If our efforts do not produce any real disciples, then we fail in our mission.

As ministers of the Gospel, when we stand before the Lord to give account of our stewardship, He will not ask how many messages we prepared. He will not be concerned about the funerals conducted, nor the potlucks where we blessed the food. He is going to ask how many disciples we helped make: *What did you do with your commission?*

If you have entered the ministry as an occupation without this commission, you will never make any disciples. The calling to make disciples, and the skills to train them, can only be imparted by the Holy Spirit. It must be alive in the heart. It is a calling from God to be a minister of the Gospel.

> "And he gave some, apostles; and some, prophets; and some, evangelists; and some, pastors and teachers; For the perfecting of the saints, for the work of the ministry, for the edifying of the body of Christ: Till we all come in the unity of the faith, and of the knowledge of the Son of God, unto a perfect man, unto the measure of the stature of the fulness of Christ."
> —Ephesians 4:11–13

First be assured you are ordained by God to this calling, and then proceed to *"Make your calling and election sure."* Rededicate yourself to the making of disciples. Understand what (or rather, who) it is you are making. Know your role in the process and hone your skills.

Take time and make sure those in leadership positions in your church have a firm understanding of Parts I and II of this manual. Ask each one specifically about their level of commitment. Do not accept placations or evasive answers. Uncover any hidden objections and address them to the point of resolution. Carefully examine the heart of each leader and make sure you have total commitment before going forward.

IMPARTING VISION TO THE CONGREGATION

Once the pastor(s) and leaders have the vision, it can then be imparted to the congregation.

The congregation does not need to know all of the details of how a disciple is made (Part II), but they should know the principles of Part I. They are: what a mature disciple looks like and the three stages of growth to get there.

When imparting the vision to become a disciple, you are actually getting people to commit to go on a journey with you. They need to know the final destination where you are going and how you intend to get them there. In other words, before they will commit to this journey, they must understand it is God's will for them to become mature disciples. They must clearly see what a mature disciple looks like (the destination). They must also have confidence that the three stages of growth are God's plan for maturity (the way to get there).

When these truths are presented properly, I have found people are more than willing to commit to the process. In some churches I have seen 100% participation—every man, woman, and child enrolled to become a mature disciple.

In order to get this level of participation from the people, some guidelines must be followed.

TAKE TIME

Take as many Sunday mornings and other meetings as needed to impart the vision. Most Christians lead a carnal life with a gloss of religion. In sharing these truths, you are reversing hundreds of years of wrong thinking and spiritual strongholds. You are setting a new definition of "normal." For some people, it will take months or possibly years to be willing to become disciples.

PREACH WITH POWER

The Bible says in Jeremiah 23:29: "'Is not my word like as a fire?' saith the LORD; 'and like a hammer that breaketh the rock in pieces?'" If you have ever broken a rock with a hammer, you know you need to hit the rock many times. In breaking these strongholds, you must speak these truths in your messages many times with great force. Come at it from different directions, but hit the mark. The Word will work, but like a hammer it must be applied forcefully.

DO THE WORK OF AN EVANGELIST

It will require the anointing of an evangelist to accomplish this work. Like an evangelist, you are changing the direction people are going and asking them to make a commitment. If you are a pastor trying to accomplish this, you will need special grace to do this work. As Paul said to Timothy: "But watch thou in all things, endure afflictions, do the work of an evangelist, make full proof of thy ministry" (II Tim. 4:5).

MAKE DISCIPLESHIP THE FOCUS OF THE CHURCH

If your congregation is accustomed to hearing different series of messages preached, they will think discipleship is just another series unless it is set apart. If discipleship is only presented as a one-time series of teachings, people will just wait for the next thing to come along. You must prove that discipleship is not going anywhere. Everyone should understand they are expected to enlist and to grow. Discipleship must become part of the DNA of the church. In order for that to happen, the vision must be clear and constantly kept in the eyes and ears of the people. Sunday messages must be preached until everyone is on board. Small groups can also meet to work through the lessons in Part I. Banners and posters portraying the three stages of growth can be displayed.

Step Two:

RECRUIT AND ENLIST DISCIPLES

THE RECRUITMENT SERVICE

Oᴎᴄᴇ ᴛʜᴇ ᴠɪsɪᴏɴ of the mature disciple is established and the three stages to maturity are understood, members of the congregation can be recruited to enlist in the process. This is done initially at a special Sunday "kick-off service." During that service, the congregation must see that you have a system in place that will:

- Evaluate them to see what stage of discipleship they have already attained and where they are in that stage.

- Recommend the course of action or training they need to progress.

- Provide sources for that training.

- Maintain accountability and support as they progress.

As can be seen from reading the following manual, the program has been simplified to a cover sheet and 4 pages. One page serves as an introduction and one page for each stage of development.

If the vision was cast properly in the preceding months, the congregation should have no problem understanding the manual and what you are trying to achieve.

NOTE: The following "Manual for Spiritual Growth" is also available for your use in MS Word format. For a free download go to *www.markswiger.org*.

(YOUR CHURCH NAME HERE)

MANUAL FOR SPIRITUAL GROWTH

"Every Member a Minister"

INTRODUCTION

The main purpose of a local church is to bring people to Jesus' salvation and then cause them to grow up to become like Him.

> "And he gave some, apostles; and some, prophets; and some, evangelists; and some, pastors and teachers; For the perfecting of the saints, for the work of the ministry, for the edifying of the body of Christ: Till we all come in the unity of the faith, and of the knowledge of the Son of God, unto a perfect man, unto the measure of the stature of the fulness of Christ."
>
> —Ephesians 4:11–13

As this scripture says: apostles, prophets, evangelists, pastors, and teachers work together to train believers to do the work of the ministry. This does not mean every member is to have a pulpit ministry, but that each believer should have the character, Bible knowledge and power of the Holy Spirit to minister where they live, work, and to the people with which they interact. All believers are called to grow to Christlike maturity.

Because of this, we require our members to grow spiritually. We are committed to insure that people can no longer attend year after year without becoming all God has called them to be.

To track your spiritual growth, we have identified the 3 biblical stages of development. They are:

- **Stage One:**   Free and Clean

- **Stage Two:**   Faithful Member

- **Stage Three:** Fruitful Disciple

Like the stages of a rocket you will grow spiritually until you are "launched" into the area of service God has called you. Completing these stages of development is the spiritual equivalent to the "basic training" that every member of our armed forces must complete. This "basic training" will equip you to serve as a "home missionary" to the people in your neighborhood, workplace, and family.

God may lead some of you to serve on a worship team, teach a Sunday school class, or disciple new converts. Some may be trained to work in a prison ministry, street evangelism, or another outreach; but *every member* will be trained and expected to serve as the "pastor" or "missionary" of where they work, study, or live.

HOW TO BEGIN

Your present stage of spiritual maturity will be determined by private interview with an ordained Minister of the Gospel. A record will be kept to track your progress. You will be able to see where you are at now and have reasonable goals set to help you become all God has called you to be.

The leaders of this church will help hold you accountable and make sure you keep growing, but the final responsibility lies with you. We will point you in the right direction and give you the support you need; but you must have the willingness, desire, and attitudes to obey and follow God.

STAGE ONE: FREE AND CLEAN

Definition: Someone who is Free and Clean is rooted and grounded in Christ. They have been "Born Again" by the Spirit of God and have obeyed the Lord in the ordinance of Water Baptism. The Free and Clean disciple has turned away from a life of sin and self-will and has demonstrated a desire to follow Jesus. Completion of the following requirements will help prove you have developed as a disciple to this stage.

REQUIREMENTS:

1. Personal evidence and testimony of salvation by the "New Birth."
   "...ye must be born again" John 3:7.

   This new birth begins with a clear commitment to Christ. The ABCs of a clear commitment is as follows:

   A. *Acknowledge* your sin and need of a Savior.

      For all have sinned and come short of the glory of God. (Romans 3:23)

      As it is written there is none righteous, no not one. (Romans 3:10)

   B. *Believe* that Jesus died on the cross to atone for your sins.

      But God commendeth His love toward us, in that, while we were yet sinners, Christ died for us. (Romans 5:8)

      But as many as received him (Jesus), to them gave he power to become the sons of God, even to them that believe on his name. (John 1:12)

   C. *Confess* Christ as your personal Lord and Savior.

      To confess means to declare publicly by speaking out freely about your repentance and faith that Jesus' death on the cross has paid for your sin (read Romans 10:8-10).

2. Water baptism by immersion subsequent to the new birth.
   ...Repent and be baptized every one of you in the name of Jesus Christ... (Acts 2:38)
   ... "Here is water; what doth hinder me to be baptized?" And Phillip said, "If thou believest with all thine heart, thou mayest"... (Acts 8:36–37)

3. Active seeking of the baptism of the Holy Ghost with the evidence of speaking in other tongues according to Acts 10:44–46.

4. Completion of a Stage One Disciples class based on teaching such as *Learning to Walk With God* by Charlie Riggs.

5. Repentance (stop doing) and deliverance (freedom) from illegal drugs and narcotics, nicotine addiction, alcohol addiction, and sexual immorality such as pornography, fornication, homosexuality, and living together without being legally married. Also things such as habitual lying, cheating and stealing, uncontrollable temper, bitterness, unforgiveness, etc.

STAGE TWO: FAITHFUL MEMBER

Definition: The Faithful Member stage of development is not to be confused with our membership in the Body of Christ, which happens when we are born again. A Faithful Member is defined here as a person who has joined this local church in particular.

A Faithful Member is someone who is Free and Clean (completed Stage One) who has made a commitment to faithfully love and serve the Lord along with the other members of this local church. Before this commitment can be entered into, there must be an agreement and understanding of the responsibilities, duties, and nature of the commitment.

> "Can two walk together, except they agree?"
>
> —AMOS 3:3

REQUIREMENTS:

1. Faithful performance of all the requirements of the Free and Clean stage for a period of at least 6 months.

2. Completion of church membership classes. These will be offered semi-annually to those who qualify. This class material will include church member conduct and behavior. Subjects to be covered will be:

    a. An overview of the church's Statement of Faith.

    b. An overview of the church's form of government and by-laws.

    c. Church discipline and conflict resolution.

    d. Teaching on the basic role and behavior expected of the member, including the member's role during worship services, preaching, and altar ministry.

    e. Faithful attendance and worship in tithes and offerings.

3. The Faithful Member must be in full agreement with the church Statement of Faith and by-laws, and must demonstrate faithfulness in attendance, tithes and offerings and in following the course of discipleship training as prescribed to them by the church.

4. The Faithful Member will also demonstrate faithfulness in worship, devotional life, and in developing and maintaining loving relationships with others.

5. Unanimous approval by the church leadership.

STAGE THREE: FRUITFUL DISCIPLE

Definition: Fruitful Disciple is hereby defined as a Faithful Member (Stage Two) in good standing, who has been trained and can function in doing "the work of the ministry." This is someone who is Spirit-filled and full of faith and zeal. They have personally "tasted and seen that the Lord is good" and heartily recommend that others do the same. They can function as the "priest of their home" and can represent Christ in the workplace and neighborhood. The Fruitful Disciple stage of development is therefore a level of personal growth in ministry.

REQUIREMENTS:

1. Faithful performance of all the requirements of Free and Clean (Stage One) and Faithful Member (Stage Two) for a period of at least one year.

2. The baptism of the Holy Spirit, with the evidence of speaking in other tongues, as in Acts 10:44–46.

3. Completion of training classes that cover the 6 "principal doctrines of Christ" as listed in Hebrews 6:1–2. These classes will be taught in a way to empower the disciple to function in these areas:
   a. Repentance from Dead Works
   b. Faith Toward God
   c. Doctrine of Baptisms
   d. Laying on of Hands
   e. Resurrection of the Dead
   f. Eternal Judgment

4. There must be evidence in the life of the Fruitful Disciple that they can serve the Lord and others by ministering salvation, physical healing, deliverance, and baptisms, all done in the Spirit of love and compassion.

5. They must demonstrate an ability to hear from God and be led by the Spirit.

6. The unanimous approval of the church-ordained ministers of the Gospel.

With completion of the above requirements, the Fruitful Disciple will be issued a card as a home missionary (or Christian Worker). This card will qualify the holder for full recognition and support in that capacity. Some Home Missionaries may also be called to serve in roles such as worship team member, Sunday school teacher, youth worker, deacon, sound system worker, elder, cell group leader, etc.

CHURCH DISCIPLINE

Should a Christian Worker fall into sin or fail to fulfill the Spirit of the various stage requirements of development, at the unanimous decision of the church-ordained ministers of the Gospel, their Christian Worker card will be revoked and they will be asked to step down from service until they fulfill a Plan of Restoration established for them by the church leaders.

FILLING OUT THE ENLISTMENT APPLICATION

After going over the manual with the congregation page by page, they need to be enlisted in the discipleship process. This is done by filling out an application.

Bringing people to this decision will take someone who is gifted in doing the work of an evangelist. You are moving them to take action and make a commitment. Only those who are skilled in the spiritual dynamics involved should attempt this. The applications should be filled out and collected before the end of the service. It should not be put off for another time.

The application should be printed on heavy cardstock so it can also serve as a record of Spiritual Growth of the disciples' progress. It should be filled out by everyone who is old enough to understand and commit to the discipleship process. (There may be exceptions, but generally age 13 and up).

I describe the level of commitment required to be a disciple to people like this: "Imagine you are living during the time of WWII. It is the day after the attack on Pearl Harbor. You are standing in line at the recruiting station. In a short time you will be signing away all rights to your life. You have resigned your job. You have kissed mother and father goodbye. You are required to enlist "for the duration," so you do not know when you will return. You may not return. You may end up buried in foreign soil, never to have had a "normal" life. Your life is not your own. Count the cost...are you still ready to sign up?"

At times I have seen 100% respond. Every man, woman, and child enlists to be trained to become a disciple like Ananias.

The Bible says: "Thy people shall be willing in the day of thy power" (Psalm 110:3).

For those who have signified they are prepared to enlist for the duration, announce that they will be contacted by a pastor.

(The following passage is from the Introduction section of this manual. I reiterate it here because this is the part of the application process where it will be put into action.)

Your present stage of spiritual maturity will be determined by private interview with an ordained Minister of the Gospel. A record will be kept to track your progress. You will be able to see where you are at now and have reasonable goals set to help you become all God has called you to be.

This would have been discussed when the manual was presented, but make sure it is announced that they will be contacted to set their appointment. They will meet with a pastor to evaluate at which stage they are and to determine a training plan.

NOTE: The following "Application for Disciple Training" is available for your use in MS Word format. For a free download go to *www.markswiger.org*.

(YOUR CHURCH NAME HERE)

APPLICATION FOR DISCIPLE TRAINING

Note: If unsure of answers leave blank.   DATE: _____ / _____
                                                        MONTH   YEAR

_____
(Last)   (First)   (Middle)

Date of Birth _____ Attending Church Since _____
                    Month/Day/Year   Year

BORN AGAIN? (Y/N) _____ Month/Year

BAPTIZED IN WATER? (Y/N) _____ Month/Year _____ ❏ Sprinkling
                                                                 ❏ Immersion

Presiding Church _____
                              (Name)   (City)

BAPTIZED IN THE HOLY SPIRIT? (Y/N) _____ Month/Year _____

   Do you or have you ever spoken in "tongues?" (Y/N) _____

MARITAL STATUS

❏ Married Anniversary _____   ❏ Single   ❏ Widowed   ❏ Married Before

Names/Ages of children living with you _____

Names of adult children _____

RELIGIOUS EDUCATION

Other churches where you were a member:

_____

Bible Classes or training you have received (Sunday school, Correspondence, Bible School, and where received)

_____

_____

_____

_____

- - - - - - - - - - - - - - (For office use only below this line) - - - - - - - - - - - - - -

❏ Born Again   ❏ Membership Class   ❏ One Year in Church
❏ Water Baptism   ❏ Agree to Statement of Faith ❏ Foundations Classes
❏ Holy Spirit Filled   ❏ Agree to By–laws   ❏ Ministry Training Classes
❏ Repentance/Deliverance   ❏ Faithful Attendance   ❏ Fruitful Disciple Stage
❏ STAGE ONE Classes   ❏ Faithful in Tithes/Offerings ❏ Licensed Christian Worker
❏ Free and Clean Stage Complete ❏ Faithful Member Stage   Card Issued

(SEE BACK OF CARD FOR NOTES/ACTIONS)

NOTES/ACTIONS

(Date and initial all entries)

DISCIPLE NAME _____

_____

_____

_____

_____

_____

_____

_____

_____

_____

_____

_____

_____

_____

_____

_____

_____

_____

_____

_____

Step Three:

EVALUATE THE RECRUITS

THE INTERVIEW

IN EVERY FIELD of education, there is first a process of testing and evaluation of those who are to be trained. For example, before being admitted to a 5th grade class, there must be proof that 4th grade class was completed. If a student has never attended school before, examinations are given to see what grade they currently function in. There are college entrance exams. There are examinations when entering the military. These are done to insure the trainee has the foundation needed to receive training. Without this it would be a waste of time and energy for both student and teacher. In some cases it could even be harmful for the student to receive knowledge without a proper framework for that knowledge.

While pre-entrance evaluations are standard in all fields of education, Christian churches seem to be the only area where this is not practiced. In a city where we once lived, my wife and I joined a growing church. We were admitted for membership without question. *The church was making members, but not disciples.* We could have attended for years, without being saved, even serving on the church worship team or in some other ministry, and our discipleship left up to time and chance.

DETERMINING THE STAGE OF GROWTH: KNOWN BY THEIR FRUITS

"Even so every good tree bringeth forth good fruit; but a corrupt tree bringeth forth evil fruit. A good tree cannot bring forth evil fruit, neither can a corrupt tree bring forth good fruit. Every tree that bringeth not forth good fruit is hewn down, and cast into the fire. Wherefore by their fruits ye shall know them."

—MATTHEW 7:17–20

There are specific signs of growth evident with each stage of development. We know people by these fruits. By conducting a private interview and asking specific questions the present stage of growth can be determined. If the stage is known then a plan for training can be determined.

PASTOR'S GUIDE TO SPIRITUAL EVALUATION

The meeting with the pastor to determine the current level of spiritual growth someone has attained is one of the most important aspects of discipleship training. It will determine what level they have already attained as well as set the course of action for their future development. It also sets the tone of their relationship to the church and its leadership. It will be a new beginning for those who are recent visitors and a fresh start for those who have attended, but never engaged.

I. ATTITUDE OF THE PASTOR

Each interview needs to be done carefully and prayerfully. Care should be taken to maintain the special and unique importance of each evaluation. This is especially true when doing large numbers of interviews. The presence and wisdom of the Holy Spirit will be needed to properly discern the true spiritual state of the parishioner. The pastor needs to be fully awake, focused, and in a position of faith so that important issues are not missed or passed over. *You should have already read the application form they filled out before the meeting. You should already have a feel for where they are at and things to address.*

II. SET THE TONE

The evaluation is not unlike getting a physical at the doctor's office. The meeting is professional and serious, but at the same time the parishioner must be made to feel at ease and comfortable. They must know you genuinely care about them and their spiritual health.

The room
Conduct the meeting in an atmosphere that speaks professionalism, but warmth. Pay attention to your manner of dress. Make sure the room is not lit too harshly to avoid an "interrogation atmosphere." Make sure the office is not too hot or too cold. Insure the meeting is not interrupted (turn off all phones!). Make sure no one enters the room. If you are evaluating someone of the opposite sex, leave the door open and have someone else in the building that can be called. Put up a "do not disturb" sign near the door. Eliminate any noises coming from outside the room.

Be efficient, but don't rush!
Never come across that you are rushing. You may need to get to the next appointment but the parishioner should never feel that. Nothing will be missed. If you feel there is more information needed, schedule another appointment.

The greeting
Take a minute or two to greet them. This is the "bedside manner" of the doctor's visit. Your body language and facial expressions will transmit much. Allow the love of Jesus to flow through you.

The transition
As you get down to the evaluation, keep the warmth yet shift to a mode that speaks professionalism and the importance of the occasion. You may want to sit behind your desk. At the minimum, the chair that you sit it and the chair they sit in should transmit who is the doctor and who is the patient.

Prayer

A short prayer will also set the tone and atmosphere. Acknowledge the presence of the Lord in the room. Underline the importance of the meeting.

III. INTRODUCING THE EVALUATION

Why you are there

Do not assume they understand why you are meeting. *Ask them if they have read the Manual of Spiritual Growth.* Explain why you need to know things about them to determine where they are at spiritually.

Confidentiality

Explain that in order to know where they are at, they need to be completely open and honest with you about their behaviors, habits, and their relationship with the Lord. Their own health and future depends on it. A doctor can't help a patient unless he knows all the symptoms. Explain that the things they share will not be disclosed to the public or to anyone they do not want to know. (Other than things that are mandatory to report in some States, such as child molestation, etc.) Only those in the ministry there that need to know will know (such as in other doctors and nurses). Your spouse may need to be in the room with you before some issues are disclosed. Some things a woman will only reveal to another woman, etc. Be sensitive to have someone else there if needed (in the same way a doctor may have a nurse in the room if examining a private area). Ask them if they would feel more comfortable if your spouse was there.

Note: Those in leadership that have access to this information must be schooled and trained on the ethics of confidentiality. If they can't keep their mouth shut, they can't be in ministry!

Line of Questioning

Remember you are there to determine if they are in Stage One, Two, or Three as a disciple. Other issues will come up that need special counseling or will need to be addressed at a later date. Make clear notes about these things, but do not try and fix them here.

Jesus said: *"By the fruits you know them."* There are identifiable fruits in people's lives that let us know who they are and where they are. The line of questioning follows Stages One, Two, and Three of a disciple examining the fruits or behaviors evident at each stage.

IV. STAGE ONE QUESTIONS

Evidence of the new birth

From the card they filled out you should see a date. Sometimes there is no clear date, only a year. There may be a range of dates. This is a sign to examine this area more closely. Sometimes people were raised in church from a child and have no clear memory of salvation. We still must determine if these people have been born again. Some questions that help explore this:

1. Tell me how you got saved.

2. What was it like before you knew Jesus? What is it like now?

3. How do you know that you were born again?

Once you are sure that they have been born again you can check that box off at the bottom of the form. *If you are unsure or if there are any doubts leave that box unchecked.*

Water Baptism by Immersion

The card should show a date and if baptized by sprinkling or immersion. If by sprinkling, you know they will need to be baptized. Also if the water baptism date predates the date they put for being born again they will need to be baptized. (This is an important area because many who struggle with besetting sin have not been baptized properly or at the proper time.)

1. Ask particulars about where they were baptized, who officiated, etc.

2. Did they believe in Jesus with all *their* heart (Acts 8:37) or did they do it because of friends, parents etc.?

If you are sure that they have been baptized properly you can check that box off at the bottom of the form. *If you are unsure or if there are any doubts leave that box unchecked.*

Baptism of the Holy Spirit with the Evidence of Speaking in Tongues

They will have answered the question on the card: *Do you speak in tongues?* An easy way to insure they are functioning at the present time is to ask them to pray in tongues along with you right then. Their baptism may be something they said a few words in the past and then stopped. In any event, if they are not fully functioning at the present time it is a sign they need more of the Holy Spirit. They need to be actively seeking.

If you are sure that they are fully functioning in tongues you can check the box off at the bottom of the form for Baptism in the Holy Spirit. *If you are unsure or if there are any doubts leave that box unchecked.*

Repentance/Deliverance

This line of questioning will reveal any besetting sin or demonic activity. Ask specific questions. Are you looking at pornography? When was the last time? Are you using any drugs? Are you addicted to prescription medication? Nicotine? Alcohol? Are you in fornication (sex outside of marriage)? Do you have anger issues? Compulsive behavior disorders? Bulimia? Anorexia? Look for areas of demonic activity. Are there any or have there been mental problems? Have they been abused? Are they free and healed from those issues?

Repeat that you can't help them if they are not totally honest with you. Jesus did not come to condemn them but to set them free. Those that are sick need a physician. Jesus is the great physician.

Ask them if there are any problem areas that you may have missed. Sins are symptoms of a relationship problem with God. We must bring these things into the light of His presence so He can cleanse and forgive.

If you are sure that they are free from besetting sin and demonic activity you can check the box off at the bottom of the form for Repentance/Deliverance. *If you are unsure or if there are any doubts leave that box unchecked.*

Have they taken the Stage One Classes?

Find out if they have taken and understand the things covered in Stage One Disciples class based on teaching such as *Learning to Walk With God* by Charlie Riggs (or similar new converts material).

(Note: If they are new babes in Christ they may be too "weak" to attend a class regularly. They may benefit from being assigned a friend to meet with them one-on-one at a convenient time and place.)

If you are confident they have already developed and are strong in this area, then grandfather them in by checking off the box. Note: There may be Stage Two people that need a refresher in these areas.

V. STAGE TWO QUESTIONS

The following questions will determine if they have developed to the Faithful Member stage or not.
   This line of questioning is to determine if the parishioner is a faithful and stable member of this local church.

1. Have they officially been accepted for membership at the church?

2. Have they read and are familiar with the church Statement of Faith and its by-laws?

    a. Are they in agreement with these?

3. Have they been faithful in tithes to this local church?

4. Have they been consistent in attendance? How long?

5. Are they consistently able to enter into worship and praise whole-heartedly during church services?

6. Do they speak in tongues freely and consistently or are they actively seeking for the same
    (filled to overflowing with the Spirit)?

7. Are they stable and consistent in personal interaction and relationships to the leadership, family
    and other members?

    a. Do they harbor any ill-will, dissatisfaction, or pains/wounds with the church leadership or any
        members of the church?

    b. Does the leadership or any members of the church harbor any ill-will, dissatisfaction, or pains/
        wounds with them?

    c. Is there a past history of going from church to church? If so has this been outgrown?

   If you are satisfied that the parishioner has grown and developed into a stable, faithful member of this local church they may be grandfathered and advanced to Stage Three training.

VI. STAGE THREE QUESTIONS

This line of questioning will determine if the parishioner has developed into the Ananias and Mark chapter 16 level of maturity and is functioning in the same.

1. Have you heard very clearly from the Lord as far as a specific direction (such as to visit this
    person, pray for that person for healing, give this certain person this message)? What were
    some of the results?

    a. How long ago?

    b. How often and consistently can you function in this way?

2. Have you led someone to accept Jesus?

    a. How long ago?

    b. Are you skilled and confident in doing this?

3. Have you prayed for someone to receive the baptism of the Holy Spirit?

    a.   If so, what happened?

    b.   Can you clearly explain to someone why they need to be filled with the Spirit, administering and leading them into that experience?

4. Have you laid your hands on the sick and seen them recover?

    a.   Tell me about your experiences.

5. Have you encountered someone that was possessed or oppressed by an evil spirit, or have you been attacked by one?

    a.   How did you handle that?

    b.   Are you skilled and confident how to handle these situations?

6. Have you ever baptized someone in water?

    a.   Do you fully understand what happened and why?

    b.   Are you confident that you can explain to someone why they need to be baptized in water and administer the same?

7. Have you ever befriended someone who was new in the Lord and met with them regularly to help them become a solid believer?

If the parishioner is fully functioning in the above and *has not slid back in the requirements of Stage One or Stage Two* they have matured to the level of a disciple. They should be issued the Christian Worker card and be officially recognized and supported by the church leadership as such.

WHEN DETERMINING STAGES

For those in Stage One, being born again, baptized in water, and filled with the Holy Spirit, if properly completed, are sufficient to make someone free and clean. However in making disciples, you will often find these things have not been completed properly. There is also a category of people who were Free and Clean but have fallen back into bondage:

> "Stand fast therefore in the liberty wherewith Christ hath made us free, and be not entangled again with the yoke of bondage."
>
>   —GALATIANS 5:1

In Stage One we also deal with people who need healing of the emotions or mind. Many have been physically or mentally abused or experienced traumas in life. Like physical healing, these areas can take time to heal. You may encounter people who have demons and need deliverance.

In making disciples it is imperative that we do not skim over this stage. If we do, their future development will be tainted. If they are allowed access to Stage Two and Three training, it is not only a bad use of time; it will be harmful to them and others.

When interviewing people in Stage Two, some may think themselves to be faithful members, but faithfulness is demonstrated by fruit over time. This must be proven by examination.

Remember, you are looking to see if there are any issues that could damage their testimony or ability to be used of God in helping others. Being free and clean, along with dependability, emotional stability and faithfulness, are the prerequisites of allowing people to progress to Stage Three training. If people who are not free and clean and faithful are allowed access to Stage Three training it will be harmful to them and others.

When evaluating people for fruit in Stage Three, you may discover those that have been doing "the work of the ministry" at some level, but who are not free and clean or faithful. There are many religious books, DVDs and audio recordings that have self-trained those who minister out of their depth. There are also churches that have empowered disciples prematurely without accountability. This can create "loose cannons" that damage the cause of Christ. Like an army of children with automatic weapons put in their hands, harm is done to the child and to the unfortunate soul that should come into contact with them.

Do not advance someone to the next stage prematurely. You will not be helping them, but keeping them from the help they need.

When evaluating disciples, you must have discernment. This work must be done with the Holy Spirit. We are looking into the souls of God's people and making life-altering decisions. We cannot do this without Him.

I have had pastors tell me the best thing they ever did in ministry was to do the one-on-one evaluations. For the first time they felt they really had a handle on things and were taking people in the right direction.

Step Four:

TRAINING THE DISCIPLES

A NEW SYSTEM OF TRAINING NEEDED

Here is an example of why current discipleship methods are not working:

Suppose you wanted to become an engineer, but you were educated under current methods of church discipleship. You might attend class for 2 hours, two times each week (Sunday morning and mid-week services). After announcements and other activities you may get 1 hour of training per class. If you attend year-round and do not miss any classes, you will receive 104 hours of training per year. Attending classes for 40 hours each week means that your school year would be over in 2½ weeks! If you do not like going to school this would seem a good thing, but if you ever wanted to be an engineer this is not so good!

Now let's add to this example the fact that your class subjects are jumbled like meetings in a church (almost every week the sermon changes to another topic). This week some math, next week hydrology, and the next physics, etc. Now imagine that students from many age groups are mixed together in your classroom (spiritual ages). Some do not qualify to be there as they never had grade school mathematics and yet others have taken the same class 10 times before!

I must also mention that this "Discipleship College of Engineering" normally has a small faculty. There is usually only 1 full-time professor (pastor). He is responsible for teaching most all of the subjects (if proficient in all areas or not). Sometimes more advanced students lead the classes and everyone tries to understand the material by open discussion (Sunday school quarterlies).

Of course people could never become engineers by using church discipleship methods. Can we expect people in this system to ever really become mature disciples of Christ?

We must return to the biblical pattern of training according to the three stages of growth. We must "redeem the time" and give training according to what is needed, who needs it, and when it is needed.

SETTING UP THE TRAINING PROGRAM

As you interview the disciples, you will begin to get a clear vision of what is needed to help everyone advance.

Classes That Repeat and Are Ongoing

Some classes will be constantly repeated as people progress through the stages and new converts are added to the church. Some of these are:

Repetitive and Ongoing for Stage One:

- The lessons for newer converts such as *Learning to Walk With God* by Charlie Riggs or the equivalent.

■ Water baptism classes and services.

■ Classes for those seeking the baptism of the Holy Spirit and "Tarrying Services."

Repetitive and Ongoing for Stage Two:

■ Membership classes that cover:

1. An overview of the church Statement of Faith.
2. An overview of the church form of Government and By-laws.
3. Church discipline and conflict resolution.
4. Teaching on the basic role and behavior expected of the member, including: the member's role during worship services, preaching, and altar ministry.
5. Faithful attendance and worship in tithes and offerings.

Repetitive and Ongoing for Stage Three:

(See the section on the "Importance of Hebrews 6:1–2 in Discipleship")

■ Completion of training classes that cover the six "principal doctrines of Christ" as listed in Hebrews 6:1–2. These classes will be taught in a way to empower the disciple to function in these areas:

1. Repentance from Dead Works
2. Faith Toward God
3. Doctrine of Baptisms
4. Laying on of Hands
5. Resurrection of the Dead
6. Eternal Judgment

SPECIALIZED CLASSES

The need for other classes will be revealed by the interviews. Many issues can be addressed in a group setting. For example, it may be revealed you have a number of people who are having problems in the marriage and family. There also may be many who are suffering from addictions. Classes may be developed just for these. The interviews may reveal a number of people who are not tithing regularly. A class on financial planning and the principles of giving in faith would be in order. The one-on-one evaluations let the leaders know what training is needed and who needs it. Specialized classes are infinitely superior to the "preach a series" method of discipleship used by many churches today. Imagine if someone were having marital difficulties. A pastor may preach a Sunday morning series every two or three years that could help their marriage, but by then they may be divorced. And how many times have we preached a message on being faithful in church attendance and the ones needing to hear it were not there! The specialized classes that come out of doing the evaluations are indispensable to making disciples.

Here are examples of the specialized classes that may be offered from time to time according to the needs of the people:

EXAMPLES OF STAGE One (Free and Clean) Specialized Classes

- Freedom from Addictions

- Repentance unto Life

- Overcoming Temptation

- Resisting the Devil

- Success over Stress

- Victory over Fears

- Be Filled with the Spirit

EXAMPLES OF STAGE Two (Faithful Member) Specialized Classes

- Godly Financial Planning

- Practicing the Presence of God

- A Life of Worship

- Cheerful Giving

- Developing a Prayer and Devotional Life

- How to Have a Happy Family

- Spouse Communication Skills

EXAMPLES OF STAGE Three (Fruitful Disciple) Specialized Classes

- Leading Others to Christ

- Healing the Sick

- Casting out Devils

- The Spirit-Led Life

- Hearing from God

- Moving in Gifts of the Spirit

INDIVIDUAL COUNSELING AND TRAINING

In addition to repeating classes and specialized classes, the evaluations will reveal private problems that can only be addressed one-on-one or are so unique a small group meeting is not justified. As pastors, the first thing we must realize is that we are not able to "fix" everybody ourselves. Most of us have not been trained or qualified to deal with many issues encountered today such as: cutting, anorexia, compulsive behavior disorders, addictions, mental illnesses, etc. We are fortunate however to have at our disposal many Christian ministries that specialize in helping people overcome these problems. There are internet-based classes, counselors, support groups, and printed materials available. We need to be Spirit-led in what we recommend and in connecting people to the right resources. The local church can help provide oversight and accountability to the disciple to make sure they keep on track.

Before you do the initial evaluations with your disciples, make sure you do "due diligence" and prepare a list of resources. You should verify that each has a high level of success. If there are any good local Christian counselors and mental health professionals in your area, contact them to develop a working relationship.

TRAINING BY STAGES...NOT BY AGES!

In most churches, training such as Sunday school is divided by children (by public school grades), teens, and adults. This is based on physical age alone. If we look into most Sunday school classrooms now, the students may all look the same age, but spiritually you will see nursery tots and the elderly all mixed together. This is not biblical and is counter-productive in making disciples.

In the Old Testament, we see a distinction between who could attend certain services. Men and women attended, and "all that could hear with understanding."

> "And all the people gathered themselves together as one man into the street that was before the water gate; and they spake unto Ezra the scribe to bring the book of the law of Moses, which the Lord had commanded to Israel. And Ezra the priest brought the law before the congregation both of men and women, and all that could hear with understanding, upon the first day of the seventh month. And he read therein before the street that was before the water gate from the morning until midday, before the men and the women, and those that could understand; and the ears of all the people were attentive unto the book of the law."
>
> —Nehemiah 8:1–3

This has been more or less adopted by Jewish tradition into the ages of 13 for males and 12 for females (Bar and Bat Mitzvahs, respectively). After this milestone, the boys and girls bear their own responsibility for obeying Jewish law and are allowed to participate in all areas of Jewish community life and adult training.

It is good to have programs for nursery and small children that are age-based. These children are not able to "hear with understanding" at a level required for discipleship training. But keeping teens separate from a mature version of discipleship not only hurts their development, but also that of the church. The Body of Christ needs the zeal and energy of youth! Some teens are more advanced in their spiritual growth than adults. They should not be held back because of age.

We face another challenge today—teens are not making the transition to adult membership. When they graduate from high school and church youth programs, the vast majority simply stop attending church altogether. Training them to become mature disciples will address this issue.

Many churches have further divided activities into other sub-groups such as young adults, single adults, and seniors. While this may or may not be advantageous for fellowship, it is not conducive to disciple making. People only have so much free time today. We must take a step back and look at the programs we offer. Is this the best use of time? Do they need this? How is this helping them become mature disciples?

THE HOLY SPIRIT AND MAKING DISCIPLES

The Holy Spirit is a very active agent in the making of disciples. He arranges situations and circumstances to give the "life lessons" needed to grow. He changes us into His image from "glory to glory" as we encounter Him.

> "But we all, with open face beholding as in a glass the glory of the Lord, are changed into the same image from glory to glory, even as by the Spirit of the Lord."
>
> —II Corinthians 3:18

Every man and woman of God has been enrolled in this "School of the Spirit." The lessons He teaches are unto life and "work together for good."

While life experiences are part of discipleship, it must never be forgotten that the primary agents the Spirit uses in making disciples are five-fold ministers and the local church. This cannot be overemphasized. Many people today have a false concept that they do not need to attend church. They feel that sitting under the pine trees with God will somehow make them mature disciples.

It is evident from Scripture that God works together with mankind to make disciples.

- When He appeared to Saul on the road to Damascus, Jesus did not instruct Saul in what he needed to do next, but sent Saul to the city where he could meet with Ananias (Acts 9:6).

- When the Angel appeared to Cornelius, he did not tell Cornelius what to do, but had him send for Peter (Acts 10:5–6).

- The Spirit told Philip to approach the Ethiopian eunuch who was reading scripture in his chariot. When Philip asked him: "Do you understand what you are reading?" the eunuch replied: "How can I, except some man should guide me?" (Acts 8:30–31).

Making disciples is not all up to man, nor all up to the Holy Spirit, but God works together with man in making disciples.

> "And they went forth, and preached every where, the Lord working with them, and confirming the word with signs following. Amen."
>
> —Mark 16:20

> "Go ye therefore, and teach all nations, baptizing them in the name of the Father, and of the Son, and of the Holy Ghost: Teaching them to observe all things whatsoever I have commanded you: and, lo, I am with you always, even unto the end of the world. Amen."
>
> —Matthew 28:19–20

WHO DOES THE TRAINING?

This is a special calling that only some are called to do.

> "And he gave some, apostles; and some, prophets; and some, evangelists; and some, pastors and teachers; For the perfecting of the saints."
>
> —Ephesians 4:11–12a

Because it takes the five-fold ministry to "perfect the saints," the maturity of a disciple is dependent upon their exposure to these offices.

There must be great change in this area of the church if we are to make mature disciples. In most churches today, the exposure of Christians to these offices is limited at best. This is due to several factors.

First, to find fully developed clergy functioning in one of these offices is rare. This harks back to discipleship and training of clergy that falls short of the mark. Next, to find five-fold ministry working together to make disciples is virtually non-existent. Some churches try to expose people to these offices by using visiting ministry. Let me just say that bringing in an evangelist or teacher for a few weeks each year is not the same thing.

Right now, you can see people that are serving in five-fold ministry, but most are serving as senior pastors. You can tell who and what they are by the fruit. A church that is known primarily for soul-winning and missions has an evangelist serving as the pastor. It is likely that if a church is known for the Word and teaching, it has a teacher serving as the pastor. If the church is known primarily for love and fellowship, then someone truly called to the office of pastor is serving as the pastor. We see people hopping from church to church today. I think they may be trying to get a "balanced diet" by exposing themselves to the different offices. God wants a local church to have all these ministries in them.

For nearly 40 years I have talked about five-fold ministry restoration: The offices working together in the local church. I have seen ministers try to unite without success. Sometimes they had partial success, but not a true five-fold ministry restoration. It would be only as "birds of a feather": prophets with prophets, teachers with teachers, pastors with pastors etc.

But now I see something different on the horizon. It is a "cloud like a man's hand" (I Kings 18:44). With it comes the abundant rain of revival. I see unity; not just for the sake of unity, but unity with a purpose: to make disciples. If the focus changes from "making meetings" to *making disciples*, ministers will unite around common ground. There is plenty of work to go around.

Five-fold ministry restoration will begin when the church begins to make real disciples. Look into your community. There are gifted men and women of God that your church members need in order to mature. They may be pastoring another church, perhaps in a different denomination. They may be on the mission field or teaching in a Bible College. They may have stepped away from ministry, burned out from struggling alone.

When I was a pastor I started a training center at the church to make disciples. For the faculty, I looked at the five-fold ministers we had at the church, but I did not limit the Lord to just them. I saw great men and women of God in the community. Each had a specific aspect of Christ that needed to be imparted. One I selected had little practical knowledge of the gifts of the Spirit, but he was a walking Bible encyclopedia. The Lord used him mightily to teach Old Testament survey. I found an elderly man of God who had evangelized in the 1960's and 70's with mighty signs and wonders. He was able to impart those qualities to the disciples.

THE ONE ROOM SCHOOLHOUSE

In the late 19th and 20th centuries, rural areas and small towns could not justify a teacher for each grade, so one teacher was hired for all levels. One-room schoolhouses were built within walking distance of the students. While more challenging for the teacher, this system worked fairly well for elementary-age students. For students needing higher education at high school and college levels, a single teacher could not give the instruction and oversight needed.

This is the same problem encountered when endeavoring to make mature disciples.

There are many "one-room churches" in operation today. To bring disciples to Christlike maturity they will need to change. If enrollments are too small to justify more ministers they could merge with other churches. A small church could also choose to work with just one aspect of disciple-making, such as working with just those in Stage One development, but they should realize where they fit in the disciple-making process. These types of ministries are not technically churches, but Bible studies, fellowships, mission outreaches, and parachurch ministries. These ministries should network with others that have a complete disciple-making vision.

Before the church where I served began making disciples, the Lord spoke to my heart: "Why should I book any passengers on your bus if you are not taking them anywhere?" When I began making disciples the Lord began adding to the church.

WORKING ALONE CANNOT PRODUCE DISCIPLES

Sixty percent of churches in the United States have less than 100 members. Ninety percent of the churches have less than 350 members. This means most churches only have one "five-fold" minister. (As mentioned before, a church that is known primarily for soul-winning has an Evangelist serving as the pastor. If a church is known for the Word and teaching it has a Teacher for the pastor. If the church is known primarily for love and fellowship, then a Pastor is serving as the pastor.)

Imagine you are the only doctor in a town within hundreds of miles. You must try to perform everything normally done in a hospital all by yourself. You do all surgeries, all diagnoses, all prescriptions, records, appointments, and counseling. You are the anesthesiologist, the x-ray technician, the therapist, and the psychologist. You change the bed-pans and mop the floors. (Welcome to the ministry!) Any doctor would soon burn-out under this pressure. But what quality of healthcare would the town receive with one physician? Only those in crisis could be cared for. This is the situation most pastors find themselves in today: crisis management. How can there be time for disciple-making?

There may still be rural places in the world where a doctor is working alone. But this scenario is something the doctor would change if at all possible. Every effort would go toward building a clinic staffed with doctors who specialize in various areas of medicine. Together they would work to create a hospital where every patient could receive the highest level of care.

A pastor working alone cannot make mature disciples any more than a doctor working alone can provide excellent health care.

MINISTERS MUST WORK TOGETHER

The Apostle Paul also knew that ministers cannot produce mature disciples by themselves. It takes ministers working together to produce mature disciples.

> "Who then is Paul, and who is Apollos, but ministers by whom ye believed, even as the Lord gave to every man? I have planted, Apollos watered; but God gave the increase. So then neither is he that planteth any thing, neither he that watereth; but God that giveth the increase. Now he that planteth and he that watereth are one: and every man shall receive his own reward according to his own labour. For we are labourers together with God: ye are God's husbandry, ye are God's building."
>
> —I CORINTHIANS 3:5–9

Notice the words in the above scripture: *"ministers.... even as the Lord gave to every man."* The Lord *gave* ministers (plural) to *every* man. This coincides with the scripture from Ephesians 4:11–12:

> ...he gave some, apostles; and some, prophets; and some, evangelists; and some, pastors and teachers; for the perfecting of the saints"

To have a plurality of ministers imparting into their lives is the God given right of every man and woman. As ministers work together to impart what we have of Christ, the image of Christ begins to appear in the lives of His people.

The Body of Christ must be re-educated to understand the importance of these offices and how they work together. Where in the Bible does it say a pastor is the head of the other offices? Why should they be compensated more financially while others live as nomads, lacking the authority and positions needed to make disciples? (Is it no wonder most everyone becomes a "pastor?") At the same time, due to wearing all 5 hats, those serving as pastors are "burning out" at an alarming rate. They may also act as bottlenecks to discipleship because everything is filtered through one office.

Making disciples together will take Christlike humility, washing each other's feet and preferring one another. It will mean a stop to *"disputing among us who will be the greatest"* (Mark 9:34). The offices must have positions of equal authority and respect if they are to function together in making disciples.

HOW THE FIVE-FOLD MINISTRY
WORKS TOGETHER TO MAKE DISCIPLES

The three stages of disciples' growth: Free and Clean, Faithful Member, and Fruitful Disciple are compared in scripture to natural growth. The Apostle John called these stages Little Children, Young Men, and Fathers. (I John 2:12–14).

Secular educational systems are usually divided into similar stages: elementary school for little children; high schools for teens (John's young men); and colleges for adults (Fathers). They have been divided this way because each stage of growth has its own unique challenges. The teachers who educate at these levels are also trained specifically for each stage. For example, a 1st grade teacher needs a different skill set to work with small children than a college professor does in working with adults. High school teachers who are dealing with problems of adolescents also need a different skill set. Not only does the knowledge of the teacher differ with each stage, but people skills change with each stage. The demeanor of first grade teachers and that of College professors must differ. Even if each teacher had the same degree and knowledge to impart, it still takes a special "gift" to work with small children, teens, or adults.

When looking at the lists of requirements and electives for disciples at Stages One, Two, and Three, a clear pattern emerges:

Stage One: Free and Clean

- Repentance from Sin

- Born Again

- Water Baptism

- Baptism of the Spirit

- Freedom from Addictions, etc.

The things disciples need at Stage One (Free and Clean), require the skill set of the Evangelist. Working with new converts requires a combination of faith and power. A new convert's faith should not be built on the Word alone, but also in power and demonstration (I Thess. 1:5).

Stage Two: Faithful Member

- Walking in agreement to Statement of Faith, etc.

- Submitting to authority

- Faithful in attendance and giving

- Faithful in relationships

- Faithful in worship and devotional life, etc.

The minister best suited to lead a disciple through this "adolescent" stage of growth would be a Pastor. Imparting faithfulness to God's people in this stage takes fatherly patience, love, and compassion. These are qualities we see in those called to pastoral work. (If pastors are free to focus on this area of expertise instead wearing all the hats, their benefit to the Body of Christ would increase dramatically.)

Stage Three: Fruitful Disciples

- The Doctrines of Christ

- Leading Others to Salvation

- Healing the Sick

- The Spirit Led Life

- The Gifts of the Spirit, etc.

Those anointed to serve in the office of Teacher would best impart these truths to disciples in Stage Three. To learn ministry skills people go to Bible colleges to be taught by teachers. But God wants all His people to have ministry skills to impact the world. They should be able to have the same (or greater) quality of training in the local church.

It is interesting that some Christian denominations have a semblance of this structure. In these organizations, an Evangelist is used to hold Gospel revivals or campaigns. Those they bring to a decision for Christ (Stage One) are encouraged to join the local church to sit under the ministry of a Pastor (Stage Two). Some of those church members would go on to Bible College for training by Teachers (Stage Three).

This has not been effective in producing mature disciples for several reasons:

1. The full work of Evangelist in helping people to be Free and Clean often takes more time than a few meetings and five minutes at an altar. Also new converts should be added to the church at all times, not just annual revivals (daily, in Scripture). They need care and oversight until they are truly Free and Clean and can progress to Stage Two.

2. Only a few members are expected to proceed to Stage Three. Since these churches only have a Stage Two vision for disciples they do not provide the training needed at the local church to become mature.

3. Many Teachers at Bible colleges and seminaries, while degreed and well intentioned, cannot impart the spiritual gifts, knowledge, and anointing of Ananias (a mature disciple).

4. Many office Teachers in the Body of Christ are serving as Senior Pastors of local churches. They are not able to focus on their callings due to the current nature of the Senior Pastor model.

THE BROWNSVILLE REVIVAL AND FIVE-FOLD MINISTRY RESTORATION

The closest thing I have seen to the offices working together to make disciples was at the Brownsville Revival in Pensacola Florida. From about 1995–2000, millions of people attended the Brownsville Assembly of God where Evangelist Steve Hill, Pastor John Kilpatrick, and Teacher Dr. Michael Brown worked together. There was much opposition from within and without to break up this partnership; and when they separated, the revival ceased.

What they experienced during the revival in Pensacola was the result of a "corporate anointing." This is a biblical principle where the sum is greater than its parts: A plurality of ministers working together creates synergy. Each of these gifted men working alone could have led a church with attendance upwards of 1000 people. *But together they impacted millions.* This is a fulfillment of Psalm 133:

> "Behold, how good and how pleasant it is for brethren to dwell together in unity! It is like the precious ointment upon the head, that ran down upon the beard, even Aaron's beard: that went down to the skirts of his garments; As the dew of Hermon, and as the dew that descended upon the mountains of Zion: for there the LORD commanded the blessing, even life for evermore."
>
> —PSALM 133:1–3

This unity is not in reference to brethren in the Body of Christ at-large, but it is the oil that ran down *Aaron's* beard: a unity of the priesthood or ministry. Notice that the Scripture says that when this unity of ministry happens, there is a Commanded Blessing of the Lord. Revival is not an option! This is what happened at Brownsville. I visited the revival near its end at the invitation of Dr. Brown. While attending I had a revelation and understood how the revival related to five-fold ministry restoration. I wrote a booklet on the subject. I was told it was well received, but forces were already in motion that destroyed their unity. I do not believe the revival was geographic. These men could have gone anywhere together and had revival.

The Lord is longing for his servants to unite and work together to make disciples.

GOVERNING BY UNANIMOUS DECISION

I have worked in several types of church governments. The one I have seen work best and I believe to be most biblical is by unanimous decision of the leaders. *This only works if the leaders are truly peers, meaning all are five-fold ministry gift office holders.* Governance with an office pastor and elected elders serving on a board will not work in this model because they are "unequally yoked."

When the leaders are truly called and gifted to a five-fold office, they are able to hear from God. If they are not able to hear clearly from God, they should not be in the ministry. In this model, I never saw discord or a situation where a full consensus could not be reached. If some were unsure about a decision, a short season of prayer and seeking God always brought harmony.

Should leadership see a pattern where someone is consistently contrary to the others, it would be like a band member who is always playing out of tune. They should be removed. At the same time, it should be understood that anyone could be out of tune once in awhile, and they should adjust if so revealed.

Rarely will you find one band-member in tune and all others off key. It is possible, but very unlikely in a group of trained professionals (truly called and gifted office ministers).

When speaking against a plurality model, a ministry that focuses on training leaders popularized the saying, "Anything with more than one head is a monster." That may true in the business world, but the head of the church is Christ. As His under-shepherds we have one head under His leadership.

THE USE OF TITLES

Titles are important when making disciples. Under the traditional pastor model, people relate the title of Pastor to an office that is over all other five-fold offices in the local church. This is harmful in a biblical disciple making model. People should understand the function and importance of each office in their development.

There are different approaches to this problem. One is that all the offices use the title of Pastor. You would still have those wanting to see the "head" or "senior pastor," but they could be directed to the "pastor" that would best answer their question or problem.

Sample:

■ Visitor: I would like to meet with the pastor.

■ Church Representative: Which one?

■ Visitor: The head pastor.

■ Church Representative: We have several that work together. What can I help you with?

Depending on the question or problem the person is routed to the pastor designated to serve in that area.

Multiple pastors will not be a problem for visitors who have attended church before, because all would have been directed to a visitor's class when they first came. They would have been told the basic disciple process and scheduled for an interview. After the interview they would have been assigned a minister to oversee them at their particular stage of development. They would know to contact that minister who would help them with their problem or direct them to someone who could.

Another option is the "Director" title. Titles could be office specific such as Director of Evangelism, Director of Pastoral Ministries, and Director of Christian Education. This would be beneficial in a larger church where there are several evangelists, pastors, and teachers in each office.

WHAT ABOUT APOSTLES AND PROPHETS?

The offices of Apostle and Prophet (not to be confused with the gift of Prophesy) are not directly involved in the day-to-day making of disciples at the local church level, but for the following purposes:

■ Mature Disciple inter-church coordination locally, regionally, nationally, and internationally.

■ Development and implementation of regional and global strategies in missions and spiritual warfare.

■ Major problem and conflict resolution.

■ Doctrinal disputes.

■ Ordination and credentialing of five-fold ministers, etc.

There are denominations that have elected officials that fill these positions. Some no longer use the titles of Apostles and Prophets, but the general roles can still be observed. Many non-denominational ministers also use the title of Apostle today. Over the years, I have observed those attempting to fill these offices. While they are doing many things that are Apostolic in nature, they are not yet functioning at the full level of gifting seen in the biblical Apostles. These offices are in the process of being restored.

To explain, I will use the analogy of the airline industry. When airplanes were few, they "barnstormed" the skies with little oversight. There were no Air Traffic Controllers or agencies to regulate them, but as airplanes increased in number, so did the need for these offices. In like manner, as churches of *mature disciples* increase in number, the office of Prophets (Air Traffic Controllers) and Apostles (Regulators) will come more into play.

I am not saying these offices are not in existence today. The manual you are reading is the result of my calling to the prophetic office. However, these offices are not yet fully functioning in the Body.

The bottom line is this: Let's first get the three offices we know about working together making disciples (Pastor, Evangelist, and Teacher). If we can't first juggle three balls how can we juggle five?

PLURALITY AND WOMEN IN MINISTRY

When the great Evangelist Reinhard Bonnke arrived in Africa with his team to conduct a major crusade, they were met at the airport by a crowd of reporters. In that nation, there was much opposition to women serving in ministry, and Bonnke had several women on his team. Thrusting microphones in his face, the reporters demanded to know why Bonnke worked with women ministers. His masterful answer completely diffused the situation in one sentence: "If I were drowning in a river, I would not care if it were a man or a woman who threw me the lifeline."

Many believers have an aversion to a woman serving in ministry. This is especially true of women who serve as lead pastors. Fear of a woman "lording it" over men has kept women from fulfilling their callings. But isn't it also unbiblical for a man to "lord it" over a congregation? Five-fold ministry restoration in the church, with Christ as the head of a plurality, will solve both of these problems.

WHAT ABOUT ELDERS?

After much study of the Scriptures, I do not believe the title "elder" in the Bible was used the same way it is today.

- The Apostle Peter called himself an elder (I Peter 5:1).

- The Apostle John called himself an elder (II John 1:1).

- The term "elders" was used in reference to the priests of Israel (Acts 4:5, 8 etc.).

- It is used to describe those serving in "five-fold" ministry. Acts 15:2, 4, 6; 20:17, etc.).

The title of church elder in Scripture meant the same thing as when we say "five-fold-minister" today. (We use the term 'five-fold' to avoid confusion.) In this light, the following scripture shows they had a plurality of five-fold ministers working together in every local church.

> "And when they had ordained them elders in every church, and had prayed with fasting, they commended them to the Lord, on whom they believed."
>
> —ACTS 14:23

THE IMPORTANCE OF IMPARTATION

One of the most powerful tools in creating disciples is the law of Impartation. The Lord uses people to impart His divine nature through the spoken Word and also through the laying on of hands. If ministers impart into believers the gifts and Christlike qualities they possess, the discipleship process is shortened by decades. Some things of God can only be received through impartation.

■ Paul imparted to the believers at Rome:

> "For I long to see you, that I may impart unto you some spiritual gift, to the end ye may be established; That is, that I may be comforted together with you by the mutual faith both of you and me."
>
> —ROMANS 1:11–12

■ The Apostles imparted to the Seven:

> "And the saying pleased the whole multitude: and they chose Stephen, a man full of faith and of the Holy Ghost, and Philip, and Prochorus, and Nicanor, and Timon, and Parmenas, and Nicolas a proselyte of Antioch: Whom they set before the apostles: and when they had prayed, they laid their hands on them. And the word of God increased; and the number of the disciples multiplied in Jerusalem greatly; and a great company of the priests were obedient to the faith. And Stephen, full of faith and power, did great wonders and miracles among the people."
>
> —ACTS 6:5–8

A person cannot give what they do not possess. I can only impart the qualities I possess that are Christlike. When selecting ministers to make disciples, I do not care how many degrees they have. I want to see what gifts and Christlike qualities they have to impart to the disciples. Paul said: "Follow me as I follow Christ."

When making disciples, the worst thing you can do is get a book on a subject and have someone lead it who has not experienced what it teaches. If you wanted to learn Judo, would you get a book and study it under someone who does not know Judo? Studying a book does not make an expert.

When it comes to imparting into the lives of disciples, it is all about what you believe and what you have become yourself. Not in repeating what someone else knows.

If Truth Is Shared Without Impartation There Will Be Inoculation

People are inoculated when they hear a truth presented without life. They then develop immunity to the real truth, thinking they have heard it before.

What You Believe in Your Heart You Can Impart

The Bible says: "Keep thy heart with all diligence; for out of it are the issues of life" (Proverbs 4:23). Life pours forth from the heart.

When making disciples we must not allow anyone to teach or preach that does not have a living Word. This is in conformance to Scripture:

> "If any man speak, let him speak as the oracles of God; if any man minister, let him do it as of the ability which God giveth: that God in all things may be glorified through Jesus Christ, to whom be praise and dominion for ever and ever. Amen."
>
> —I PETER 4:11

THE IMPORTANCE OF HEBREWS 6:1–2 IN DISCIPLESHIP

After I graduated from Bible school in 1977, my wife and I took our 6-month-old baby girl and moved to the State of Montana to pioneer a church. Not long after a close friend of mine in the ministry came for an extended visit.

One day he asked me a question: "How well do you know the doctrines of Christ listed in Hebrews chapter 6?" I replied that the teachers I had in Bible School had addressed them somewhat, but I knew little about them myself. I had to admit my knowledge was limited to parroting the things I heard the teachers say.

He then told me some things about the doctrines that revealed I only knew a little bit of what was available. He explained to me that very few ministers, in fact a tiny percentage, are taught by God about these 6 subjects. He advised me to seek God for myself and cry out to God for understanding. I took this challenge very seriously and applied myself. What I learned had life-changing impact on myself and on the multitudes my ministry touched over the years.

> "Therefore leaving the principles of the doctrine of Christ, let us go on unto perfection; not laying again the foundation of repentance from dead works, and of faith toward God, Of the doctrine of baptisms, and of laying on of hands, and of resurrection of the dead, and of eternal judgment."
>
> —HEBREWS 6:1–2

The first thing to notice is that these 6 doctrines are the doctrines or teachings of Christ Himself. These are the subjects Jesus taught His disciples in His "Walking Bible School"! When doing pastors' seminars, I ask the pastors: "What are the 6 subjects Jesus taught His disciples?" Always less than 3 out of 100 pastors know the answer. (Most of the time no one knows unless I give some hints.)

These teachings, when properly understood and believed, are foundational and formational in making disciples. You cannot make a disciple without them. It is impossible to bring a disciple to "perfection" (full growth) unless this foundation has been properly laid.

They are:

1. Repentance from Dead Works

2. Faith Toward God

3. Doctrine of Baptisms

4. Laying on of Hands

5. Resurrection of the Dead

6. Eternal Judgment

What you believe about the first two: (Repentance from Dead Works and Faith Toward God) Determines *Who* You Are.

What you believe about the next two: (Doctrine of Baptisms and Laying on of Hands) Determines *What* You Do.

What you believe about the last two: (Resurrection of the Dead and Eternal Judgment) Determines *Why* You Do It.

This is why these truths are so critical, and why the enemy has attacked them for millennia. They are what create, empower, and motivate the disciple. These are the doctrines that the disciple Ananias was taught. They caused him to become the mighty man of God revealed in Scripture.

When I first began seeking the Lord on these subjects, I found only two books had been written. One called *Laying the Foundation* by James Beal and the other a collection of teachings transcribed from the radio program of Derek Prince entitled *Foundational Truths for Christian Living.* While reading these was beneficial, I did not receive the heart knowledge I needed to impart into the lives of others until I sought the Lord for understanding myself. He showed me things in a way that came alive in me. I could then impart these life changing truths to help make disciples.

> "Yea, if thou criest after knowledge, and liftest up thy voice for understanding; If thou seekest her as silver, and searchest for her as for hid treasures; Then shalt thou understand the fear of the LORD, and find the knowledge of God."
>
> —PROVERBS 2:3–5

The 6 doctrines of Christ will produce mighty disciples, but to be imparted they must be alive in the heart of the ones doing the discipling.

- Because Peter believed the doctrine of Repentance from Dead Works in his heart, he was able to stand up on the day of Pentecost and declare it in power. Thousands responded to that living Word.

- The Apostle Paul believed the doctrine of Eternal Judgment. It was living in him so that when he talked of it to Felix, the Bible declares Felix "trembled".

- The disciple Ananias didn't just have "head knowledge" about the doctrine of Laying on of Hands. When Ananias laid his hands on Saul, the scales fell from his eyes.

The truths of Hebrews chapter 6 are so powerful that entire Bible schools have been built around just one of them. The disciple that has all 6 imparted will have a much better foundation and Bible knowledge than today's seminary graduate.

> "And the things that thou hast heard of me among many witnesses, the same commit thou to faithful men, who shall be able to teach others also."
>
> —II TIMOTHY 2:2

These wonderful truths should only be imparted to faithful people. I have had great results when only Faithful Members (Those who have completed Stage Two) are allowed access into the Hebrews 6 classes. I will not empower the unfaithful or the unclean.

God is no respecter of persons. The God who made the doctrines of Christ come alive in me will do so for other men and women of God. God is raising a multitude of men and women who can impart these truths to the Body of Christ. Some will cry out to God and obtain these heavenly treasures. Many will sit under anointed ministers who can impart a living Word into their souls. They in turn can teach others. I pray many will hear this exhortation and not settle for parroting another man's words.

SUNDAY MORNING SERVICE AND DISCIPLESHIP

As mentioned in a previous lesson, making mature disciples will necessitate many changes in how we "do church." This also includes changing the order of Sunday Morning services.

For most churches, the primary vehicle used in teaching Christians is the pastoral Sunday morning message. This will not work in training disciples, and here is why:

Back when I attended grade school, sometimes there would be a "General Assembly" when all the grades would gather in the Gymnasium. Every student from Kindergarten to 6th grade would be there. The principal would usually oversee the meeting. We would sing some "pep rally" songs or seasonal Christmas carols. There would be announcements that concerned the student body. Sometimes one of the classes would do skits or songs, or a special speaker such as a police officer would give a talk on safety that we all could understand. But the principal did not try to teach during the General Assembly. This is because many age groups were present. If the principal attempted to teach on a subject, say mathematics, only a small percentage of the students could learn at one time. For the vast majority, any information would be either beyond their level of understanding or something they already knew. Using that format would be a waste of training time and energy, both for student and teacher. For this same reason, the "General Assembly" of church on Sunday morning cannot be the primary mode used in teaching disciples.

Also, for reasons previously stated, information given at the wrong time to the wrong people can damage them. Unless built upon a solid foundation, a little knowledge can be worse than none at all.

This is why Jesus did not use mass meetings that were open to the general public to train disciples. They did however serve important functions. Mass meetings are used in the Bible for:

- Evangelism in calling people to repentance and to accept Jesus as Savior

- Healing and Deliverance

- Signs and Wonders

- Prophetic Words to the Body

- Outpourings of the Holy Spirit

- A Message that is suitable for the unsaved and all spiritual ages (As when Jesus spoke in parables, but later disclosed the deeper meaning to the disciples in private. See Matthew 13:11)

- Praise and Worship

- Communion

- Meals and Fellowship

- Announcements

As students in grade school, we understood the General Assembly was only a small part of attending school. We must break the stronghold in the minds of Christians today that think the General Assembly is what church is all about. To change this mind-set and start making mature disciples, we must stop making the Sunday morning pastoral message the venue for discipleship in the church.

To do this we must understand why and how the Sunday message became central to discipleship in the first place.

THE CATHOLIC MASS

There are variations according to liturgical season, but Roman Mass or Eucharist celebrations follow this general pattern:

1. INTRODUCTORY RITES:
   - The Entrance of the Priest/Processional
   - The Greeting/Opening Prayers/Blessing
   - Congregational Singing such as "The Gloria in Excelsis" (Glory to God in the Highest)
   - Prayer

2. LITURGY OF THE Word:
   - Three scripture readings, one from:
     - The Old Testament Followed by Psalms
     - The New Testament
     - The Gospels
   - A Sermon or Homily given by the priest that draws upon the scripture that was read
   - All recite the Nicene Creed or Apostles Creed/Prayer by the priest

3. LITURGY OF THE Eucharist:
   - Ceremonial Placement of Bread and Wine/Eucharist Prayer by Priest and Congregation
   - Consecration
   - Doxology
     - Communion Rite:/Distribution of Communion
     - Prayer after Communion

4. CONCLUDING RITE:
   - Announcements
   - Priest's Blessing
   - Priest and ministers leave to recessional hymn
   - Congregation departs
   - Priest stands by church exit door to greet people individually

"From roughly the time of St. Gregory [d. 604] we have the text of the Mass, its order and arrangement, as a sacred tradition that no one has ventured to touch except in unimportant details."
—FR. ADRIAN FORTESCUE,
THE MASS: A STUDY OF THE ROMAN LITURGY [1912]

The Catholic mass is based on the Gospel accounts of the Lord's Supper and other Scriptural references to taking communion. While insightful for communion services, these scriptures were not intended to be used as the basis for disciple training.

What is fascinating in studying the order of Catholic Mass is that virtually all churches and denominations follow the same general format on Sunday morning. That being:

1. Introductory Greetings and Prayers

2. Congregational Singing

3. Sermon

4. Communion (some on a monthly basis)

5. Dismissal

Language used in Protestant churches has been modernized. The songs have also changed and the services more flexible, *but the same basic pattern is used to conduct meetings.* The only major change is the sermon became more dominant in churches where emphasis shifted away from the Eucharist (Communion).

This Sunday sermon format was developed in a time when people could not read and had no Bibles. The priest would read a section from the Old and New Testaments, the Psalms and Gospels. He would then give a sermon based on the reading. This would be done in an annual system so people were exposed to the Scripture in a methodical way. Think of the millions of Christians in church today whose discipleship training is almost entirely dependant on a system developed in the dark ages for the illiterate.

The Catholic order of services on which we have based our church meetings is not able to produce disciples. Jesus did not command us to "Go into all the world and make meetings," but to make disciples. We need to take a step back and look at our meetings in the light of making disciples.

The mass meeting or "General Assembly" should be used for the same purposes that Jesus did, but not as the vehicle for training disciples.

ORDER OF SUNDAY SERVICE IF BASED ON DISCIPLE-MAKING

An order of service for Sunday that is based on disciple-making would look more like this:

- Welcome Greeting and Opening Prayer

- Announcements

- Tithes and Offerings

- A Special song or Hymn

- Dismissal to Discipleship Classes assigned according to the three Stages of Development and electives.

- (Infants and Children under 13 dismissed to age-based programs)

- Visitors would be directed to a place to be welcomed, to learn about the church and be plugged into the discipleship program. (Fill out Discipleship Application and appointment for evaluation.)

- Return of the Congregation for Worship Service, Communion if so led, manifestations of the Holy Spirit and gifts, testimonies, signs and wonders, and Spirit-led prayer. Preaching (if any) should be done prophetically as instructed in scripture *"If any man speak, let him speak as the oracles of God"* (I Peter 4:11a). Those doing ministry should be limited to disciples who have matured to at least Stage Two (Disciples who are free and clean) and five-fold ministers.

- Closing Prayer and Dismissal

If Sunday morning sermons are not used to train disciples, the General Assembly on Sunday can instead focus on the manifestations and operation of the gifts of the Holy Spirit. The services will then be conducive to fulfill:

> "But if all prophesy, and there come in one that believeth not, or one unlearned, he is convinced of all, he is judged of all: And thus are the secrets of his heart made manifest; and so falling down on his face he will worship God, and report that God is in you of a truth."
>
> —I Corinthians 14:24–25

LIMITING BODY MINISTRY TO FREE AND CLEAN DISCIPLES AND "FIVE-FOLD" OFFICES

When people gather together they have a right to a safe environment. If we allow everyone to minister in our services, we open the door to anyone. I have seen covens send witches into services to "pray for people" and disrupt services. Child molesters have joined churches volunteering to teach Sunday schools and lead youth groups. Often churches that provide an environment open to the moving of the Spirit will have visitors attending who are "loose cannons." They feel they are sent as prophets to the Body of Christ at-large with a "Word from the Lord." Often they have left other churches because of problems in submitting to authority (failed in Stage Two).

A discipleship system need not "put God in a box" or limit the moving of the Holy Spirit. The evaluation and discipleship process allows us to "prove all things." Any reasonable person wanting to serve God would gladly meet with the pastor for spiritual evaluation. If they are truly mature and functioning in the Gifts of the Holy Spirit, it will stand up to examination. Time should be taken to verify statements, observe behavior, and check backgrounds. If they are truly sent by God, they can be grandfathered in and licensed as Christian Workers or in a five-fold ministry office.

In every Spirit-led church there are always adolescent believers who, like teenagers, cry for their freedom, rights and the "liberty of the Spirit." Just ask them if they would like a witch or demon-possessed person to lay hands on them in church. Some may kick at restrictions, but in the end the church leadership will be respected for providing a safe environment where the Holy Spirit is still free to move.

THE USE OF SMALL GROUPS AND HOME MEETINGS

Small groups and home meetings can be indispensable in making disciples, *but not if they are mini-versions of traditional church services*. These groups should be used for specialized training that is stage-specific to the needs of the people.

Home groups can also serve as meeting places for Christian Workers (Those who have completed Stage Three training) to coordinate evangelism and ministry outreach programs into the community.

But there is also another very important use of homes in making disciples: *Their daily use.*

> "And they, continuing daily with one accord in the temple, and breaking bread from house to house, did eat their meat with gladness and singleness of heart, Praising God, and having favour with all the people. And the Lord added to the church daily such as should be saved."
>
> —ACTS 2:46–47

> "And daily in the temple, and in every house, they ceased not to teach and preach Jesus Christ."
>
> —ACTS 5:42

When my wife and I were saved back in 1974, we came out of the drug culture. We were accustomed to being with our "hippy friends" and hanging out on the street. As soon as we came to Christ, all of our so-called friends deserted us. We had no place to go and nothing to do, but go to church. We loved being part of the church, but we only met there three times a week. We were still "babes in Christ" with a lot of time between services to be tempted to fall back into our old lifestyle.

Thank God there was a married couple in the church who opened their hearts and home to us. It seems we were over at their house 24/7. Looking back, you would think they would have gotten tired of us, feeling indisposed or taken advantage of. If they ever did feel that way, they never let us know. Even though they had small children and the husband worked full time, we were always welcome. We fellowshipped, talked about the things of the Lord, and conversed about many subjects. We ate a whole lot of meals and pizzas. We spent an entire year hanging around their house until we were strong enough in the Lord where we did not need constant care. In retrospect, we probably would have backslid and gone to hell if not for them. (We will never forget you, Mike and Pat Morast.)

This is likely the most important use of homes in making disciples. Not just in having scheduled meetings and classes, but the home of the mature believer should be a place where people are welcome any time of the day or night, "breaking bread from house to house." As disciples mature in your church, there can be dozens and ultimately hundreds of these homes spread throughout the city. Places where people can be loved and accepted. Places of fellowship and healing....a living church that never closes its doors.

> "By this shall all men know that ye are my disciples, if ye have love one to another."
>
> —JOHN 13:35

Step Five:

ACCOUNTABILITY AND DISCIPLINE

RECORD KEEPING

"Obey them that have the rule over you, and submit yourselves: for they watch for your souls, as they that must give account, that they may do it with joy, and not with grief: for that is unprofitable for you."

—Hebrews 13:17

A SYSTEM OF ACCOUNTABILITY must be in place in making disciples. Those in ministry are first and foremost accountable to God. We are assigned the awesome task of watching over souls. This responsibility is similar to that in a doctor-patient relationship. Ministers are charged with people's eternal spiritual health and growth. Each person must be cared for as a precious individual. Nobody should "fall through the cracks." Everyone should receive the same level of care despite wealth or social status.

Most would agree the eternal soul is more important than the temporal body, yet some ministers approach the care of souls in a way that would be called malpractice in medicine. Usually few if any records are kept and a person can attend church for years, perhaps a lifetime, without a spiritual check-up or examination. Some only see the pastor when near death or at their funerals (spiritually and physically).

It is interesting to note that records are kept on the people of God:

- In the Old Testament

- In the New Testament Church

- In Heaven

As in physical care, spiritual care requires having a system for examination, observing symptoms (fruit), prescribing a course of action, and tracking set backs or improvements.

The following appears on the bottom of the Application For Disciple Training. This is provided as a suggestion for a record system.

--------------------------------- (For office use only below this line) ---------------------------------

❏ Born Again	❏ Membership Class	❏ One Year in Church
❏ Water Baptism	❏ Agree to Statement of Faith	❏ Foundations Classes
❏ Holy Spirit Filled	❏ Agree to By-laws	❏ Ministry Training Classes
❏ Repentance/Deliverance	❏ Faithful Attendance	❏ Fruitful Disciple Stage
❏ Stage One Classes	❏ Faithful in Tithes/Offerings	❏ Licensed Christian Worker
❏ Free and Clean Stage Complete	❏ Faithful Member Stage	Card issued

(SEE BACK OF CARD FOR NOTES/ACTIONS)

This application would be printed on heavy cardstock in order to serve as a record of the disciple. The column on the left corresponds with the basic requirements of Stage One found in the manual, the middle column Stage Two, and the one on the right Stage Three. When all boxes are "ticked" the disciple would be acknowledged as a Christian worker. The back of the card would serve as a place to record special circumstances and actions taken in training the disciple.

A card file should be kept on every disciple. Strict access and confidentiality must be observed in keeping these records. Some churches have optioned to computerize the information and password-protect the files.

It should be noted that both this Manual and the Application can be modified to suit a particular church culture or program. These are provided as a guide. Some churches have elected to use them without modification.

WHO IS RESPONSIBLE TO OVERSEE THE DISCIPLE?

"Obey them that have the rule over you, and submit yourselves: for they watch for your souls…"
—HEBREWS 13:17a

We have already established that making disciples is not a one-person job. To mature disciples the offices of Evangelist, Pastor, and Teacher should have part in their development at the local church level. There must be excellent communication between these offices to avoid conflicting counsel and duplication of effort. This also underlines the need for a record system.

In the medical profession, doctors with different specialties may treat the same patient. All doctors would have access to the patients "chart" or records, but there is one who is responsible as the primary physician. The minister primarily responsible for a disciple's care may change over time and with each stage of development, but it must be clear who is in charge of overseeing the disciple at any given time.

TIP: I have found disciples in-training can be like children who go from parent to parent until they get the answer they want to hear. Ministers must communicate closely together to keep the disciple from playing them off each other.

MENTORING THE DISCIPLES

I am going to recommend a system to oversee the disciples. This is not cast in stone, but I submit it for consideration in the same framework the Apostle Paul offered advice in I Cor. 7:40:

"…after my judgment: and I think also that I have the Spirit of God."

The initial interview to classify the disciple as Stage One, Two, or Three should be completed by someone in the pastoral office. Pastors by nature of their gift have the "bedside manner" best suited to accomplish this part of the work (Pastors not just in title, but having the gift of the office).

If someone is classified in Stage One, I would designate someone gifted in the office of an evangelist to oversee or mentor that disciple until they are Free and Clean. As they progress through Stage Two, (or are grandfathered) a pastor would best oversee the disciple in this Faithful Member stage. As they receive training in Christian Worker Stage Three, someone gifted as an office teacher would take the oversight.

Experience has taught me that a minister cannot effectively oversee the growth of more than 100 disciples at a time. This means that if there are more than 100 in any stage, another minister would be added. So if there are 200 disciples in Stage Two development, there would be 2 pastors. If there are more than 100 in Stage Three, an office teacher would be added per 100 for disciple oversight purposes. Again, the classes the ministers teach and where they are best utilized is determined by the disciple interview process.

NOTE: *Even though the minister is providing oversight, avoid using the title of "overseer" as it can have negative connotations in our society. The generic term pastor is more suitable.*

I was told at the height of the Brownsville revival in Pensacola there were 70 pastors working under Pastor Kilpatrick and 14 full-time teachers under the office of teacher Dr. Michael Brown. I was not told the number of those working under the direction of evangelist Steve Hill, but I imagine there was work for many ministers following up on decisions, baptisms, setting the captives free, etc.

The oversight of disciples once they complete Stage Three (Fruitful Disciple) and are fruitful in ministry would be a function of the Apostolic and Prophetic Offices. Oversight at this level is general and supportive in nature. Oversight of a *mature disciple* is about networking them with other disciples and ministries, mentoring them if they are called to five-fold ministry, and developing Holy Spirit strategies to coordinate the mature disciples locally, regionally and globally, etc.

OVERSIGHT CHANGES WITH MATURITY

At each stage, the amount of oversight reduces and the relationship with the "overseer" changes. As children become adults, the relationship with their mother and father changes. They no longer raise their hands at the dinner table and ask if they may be excused. Parents no longer tell them: "You can't get up until you eat everything on your plate!" Leadership must also adjust as disciples mature. Mature disciples will leave the local church unless they have respect and support to function. Fellowship must be maintained and the family structure preserved without mature disciples feeling they must leave the local church.

When making disciples, producing people who know God for themselves should remain the objective. You can see this in the ministry of John the Baptist. John had many disciples that followed him. He had led a major revival and had a large ministry. As Jesus began his ministry, John's disciples left him to follow Jesus. John wrote:

> "He that hath the bride is the bridegroom: but the friend of the bridegroom, which standeth and heareth him, rejoiceth greatly because of the bridegroom's voice: this my joy therefore is fulfilled. He must increase, but I must decrease."
>
> —JOHN 3:29–30

As ministers of the Gospel and "friends of the bridegroom," it should also be "our joy" to lead people into a deep relationship with the Lord. Making disciples is about leading people into intimacy with the Lord and taking a lesser role as they mature. "He must increase and I must decrease."

DISCIPLINE AND DISCIPLES

A system of accountability includes how and when to discipline. In the early church discipline was sometimes very severe. When Ananias and his wife Sapphira (Acts chapter 5) sold property and gave an offering to the church, they held back part of the money for themselves. They lied and said they donated the entire proceeds of the sale. This cost them their lives. (Today Ananias and Sapphira would likely not have been killed, but would have a brass plaque on the church wall in honor of their large contribution!)

We also see a church instructed to discipline a member who sinned in this way: "deliver such a one unto Satan for the destruction of the flesh, that the spirit may be saved" (I Cor. 5:5). (When is the last time you went to church and heard the announcement, "OK...we are going to pray and turn Brother Joe over to Satan now.")

I do not believe this means the Lord has relaxed His standards in our day. The Bible says the Lord changes not. What have changed since Bible days are the "open heaven" of revival and maturity of the disciples. The Bible declares to whom much is given much is required, and much was given to the early church.

In our legal system, maturity is also a factor in punishment. A 12-year-old may commit a crime that would result in a death sentence if he were 18 years old, but because of his lack of maturity he could be released after staying in a juvenile home. In the same way, God disciplines His children according to their circumstances and level of maturity.

In discipline, we must remember we are likely not dealing with mature disciples. God is longsuffering. He is merciful and kind. Slow to anger. We must deal softly with God's children, not calling down fire from heaven in the wrong spirit like James and John would have done (Luke 9:54).

The heart of God in dealing with people in sin can be seen in Matthew 18:15–17:

> "Moreover if thy brother shall trespass against thee, go and tell him his fault between thee and him alone: if he shall hear thee, thou hast gained thy brother. But if he will not hear thee, then take with thee one or two more, that in the mouth of two or three witnesses every word may be established. And if he shall neglect to hear them, tell it unto the church: but if he neglect to hear the church, let him be unto thee as a heathen man and a publican."

God wants as few people as possible to know about our faults. This is to preserve our testimony and future use in the Kingdom.

> "Brethren, if a man be overtaken in a fault, ye which are spiritual, restore such a one in the spirit of meekness; considering thyself, lest thou also be tempted."
> —GALATIANS 6:1

It is God's desire that people be restored if at all possible. When a disciple becomes a member in Stage Two, part of that process is that they agree to your system of discipline and resolving conflicts. This keeps them from leaving the church without some dialog. I have found a written "plan of restoration" is helpful in many cases. For example, say someone on the worship team falls into sexual sin. Keep the matter as private as you can, but if the sin is a public matter the church will need to know you are dealing with it in a loving and restorative way. Develop a plan of restoration approved by the other church ministers. The plan would probably include repentance, stepping down from the worship team for a set time, counseling etc. I found if the plan is put into writing and the disciple signs the plan there can be restoration.

When they refuse to sign…watch out! In most every case, they will go on the attack to discredit the church. I call it the "get them before they get me" response. They will spread some lies about the church and the leaders to draw attention away from their sin. The Bible says in this case to "mark them."

> "Now I beseech you, brethren, mark them which cause divisions and offences contrary to the doctrine which ye have learned; and avoid them."
> —ROMANS 16:17

You can "mark" someone by a simple announcement to the church. Something like: "You may have heard Brother Joe has fallen into sexual immorality. We have tried to restore him to full fellowship, but he is not repentant and has left the church. Please keep him in prayer." You do not want to "mark" someone unless absolutely necessary as it will impact their future ministry. On the other hand, not "marking" someone can often cause damage to the church.

A worship leader in our church had fallen into sin and refused to agree to the "Plan of Restoration" developed by the leadership. Instead he began calling and visiting other church members to say how he was mistreated and asked to step down from ministry without cause. Not wanting to "mark" him publicly we delayed action for several weeks. We lost several families to his lies before we informed the church of our efforts to restore him.

In a family, disciplining children takes wisdom, consistency, fairness, and love. Often the welfare of the entire family is a factor. This is why ruling your own house well is mandatory for those serving in the ministry. Both require the same skill set.

> "One that ruleth well his own house, having his children in subjection with all gravity; (For if a man know not how to rule his own house, how shall he take care of the church of God?)"
> —I Timothy 3:4–5

Make sure you have a written policy for disciple discipline in place. The disciples should read, understand, and agree to this policy as they enter Stage Two.

Step Six:

RECOGNITION AND SUPPORT

HONOR ONE ANOTHER

While we are told the motivation for our good deeds is not to be seen of men, the Bible encourages us to honor each other.

Romans 13:7 instructs us to give "honor to whom honor" is due.

> "Let the elders that rule well be counted worthy of double honour, especially they who labour in the word and doctrine."
>
> —I Timothy 5:17

> "Be kindly affectioned one to another with brotherly love; in honour preferring one another."
>
> —Romans 12:10

> "Who also honoured us with many honours; and when we departed, they laded us with such things as were necessary."
>
> —Acts 28:10

> "Honour all men. Love the brotherhood. Fear God..."
>
> —I Peter 2:17a

> "Or unto governors, as unto them that are sent by him for the punishment of evildoers, and for the praise of them that do well."
>
> —I Peter 2:14

According the above verse God sent governors, not only to punish evildoers, but also to praise those who do well. God is evidently not against praising those who do well. Honoring someone for their accomplishments not only benefits them, but the entire church as it rejoices with them:

> "And whether one member suffer, all the members suffer with it; or one member be honoured, all the members rejoice with it. Now ye are the body of Christ, and members in particular."
>
> —I Corinthians 12:26–27

As disciples progress, there are milestones of achievement that must be recognized and celebrated for the benefit of all.

MILESTONES OF DISCIPLES

In Stage One (Free And Clean)

- Healings and Deliverance from Possession or Oppression

- Salvation (Born Again)

- Water Baptism

- Baptism of the Holy Spirit

- Completion of "Learning to Walk with God" Class (or equivalent)

- Acceptance for Church Member Training (Promotion to Stage Two)

In this early stage of development, a disciple needs the level of encouragement a small child would receive. This is especially true when it comes to praise and recognition. Any healing, both physical and spiritual, triumph over addictions; salvation and other such victories should be acknowledged and celebrated. This can be done in the form of testimony by the disciple in a General Assembly. Public confession of Christ's work not only substantiates it in the soul of the disciple, but edifies the church. A benefit of having a minister "watch over the soul" of each disciple is that these events are known and the disciple can be encouraged to testify.

Water baptism and baptism of the Holy Spirit should be recognized publicly. Completion of classes should be acknowledged formally by awarding certificates before the congregation.

The promotion of the disciple to Stage Two training as a Faithful Member is an accomplishment that should be celebrated in a major way. This acknowledges the disciple has truly become Free and Clean: spirit, soul, and, body. Unsaved family members and loved ones should also be invited to celebrate at this event.

NOTE: There is often inequality in how we celebrate in church culture. For example, when someone turns a year older, we give gifts and invite friends to a party. But when someone receives eternal salvation, the Holy Spirit or miraculous healing there is often a dull reaction. When in India, I saw the Lord heal a woman who walked for the first time in 30 years. Her village invited the surrounding villages to a party that lasted three days. I thought, "Now that is an appropriate response!" Let's react properly to what God is doing.

IN STAGE TWO (FAITHFUL MEMBER)

- Having stayed Free and Clean

- Completion of Membership Classes

- Acceptance as Members

- Having been proven Faithful in Attendance, Giving, Prayer, Worship, Devotional Life and Relationships

- Acceptance for Disciple Ministry Training (Promotion to Stage Three)

For disciples who were former addicts, staying Free and Clean for even a few weeks or months is a cause for celebration. Any completion of classes should be acknowledged formally by awarding certificates before the congregation. When the disciple is accepted as a member of the church it should be done officially before the congregation. Part of that service should go over both the responsibility the disciple has to the church and that of the other members to the disciple. As in promotion to Stage Two, promotion to Stage Three should be celebrated in a major way. This acknowledges the disciple has truly become a faithful person and can be trusted to be equipped for ministry. Unsaved family members and loved ones can also be invited to celebrate at this event.

IN STAGE THREE (FRUITFUL DISCIPLE)

■ Having stayed Free and Clean and Faithful

■ Completion of the Doctrines of Christ Hebrews 6 Classes

■ Having been Trained and Equipped for Ministry

■ Having been proven Fruitful in Ministry

■ Has been Licensed/Ordained as a Christian Worker (Fruitful Disciple)

Fewer public awards are needed as disciples mature and function in ministry as Ananias. What should be formally recognized in this stage is that the disciple has completed basic ministerial training and can be licensed; and after the disciple has proven fruitful in ministry, upgraded to ordination. This is important because by doing so the leadership is giving their stamp of approval for the mature disciple to:

■ Lay hands on the sick

■ Operate in Gifts of the Spirit

■ Comfort and Exhort

■ Open their home for fellowship

■ Perform ministry as demonstrated by Ananias both in the church and without

By public acknowledgment and credentialing the congregation knows that this person is free and clean, faithful, and can be trusted to minister in the love and Spirit of Christ. It would not be unscriptural for the disciple to be conferred the title of "Minister" at this point.

■ NOTE: *It should be underlined that disciples are not authorized to rebuke or reprimand people. This is a special authority reserved for those in five-fold office, as Paul authorized Timothy and Titus (Titus 2:15, I Timothy 5:20).*

The mature disciple should always focus on encouraging, building up and comforting others (I Cor. 14:3). The only exception to this in scripture is when the disciple has been personally sinned against.

> "Take heed to yourselves: If thy brother trespass against thee, rebuke him; and if he repent, forgive him."
>
> —LUKE 17:3

SUPPORT OF THE MATURE DISCIPLE (CHRISTIAN WORKER)

Over the last two millennia, there have been churches where disciples demonstrated aspects of Christlike maturity. There were revivals where disciples worshiped in Spirit and truth, churches where fervent prayer was common, where healing, joy, prophecy, or other aspect of Christ was observed in many disciples at the same time. What we have not seen is the fulfillment of Ephesians 4:13:

> "Till we all come in the unity of the faith, and of the knowledge of the Son of God, unto a perfect man, unto the measure of the stature of the fulness of Christ."

As disciples mature to the level demonstrated by the disciple Ananias, a situation will arise that current church leadership is not prepared for- how to relate to a church full of mature disciples.

I think the answer will be in the relationship that good parents have with their adult children. Do not micromanage or control them. Let them go and give them freedom to live their own lives. Be there for support if needed and advice if asked. Love them and be proud of their accomplishments. Pray for them.

Church for mature disciples should be different than when they were "babes in Christ." Church should not remain a school where they perpetually take classes over and over again. There must be a graduation. There must be a commencement. There must be a release.

Mature disciples should not be burdened with meetings that take them away from productive service. Any meetings should be for the purposes of coordinating God-given strategies to reach the community, to give praise reports of the exploits being done, to give refresher training if needed, to maintain unity, fellowship, and networking between disciples or for corporate worship and prayer. Church for the mature disciple would look more like a ministerial fellowship or association.

Mature disciples should first and foremost be encouraged to use their abilities to impact the community, co-workers, neighbors, and family members. Some workers may be used to serve in ministries needed around the church, but this should be done carefully and sparingly to not direct energies inwardly. The first priority of the disciple is to *turn the world upside down.*

DISCIPLES CALLED TO FIVE-FOLD MINISTRY

Some mature disciples may be called to the five-fold ministry. This is not the normal path for the Christian and is not the "next level" of growth. This is a specific calling from the Lord and should always be the exception and not the rule.

The worst thing we can do to a disciple is to put them in five-fold ministry when there is no calling. They will suffer and the Body will suffer loss. Because a mature disciple is so much more powerful than the "Average Christian" seen today in the Body of Christ, the temptation will be for them to stand in an office they are not called to. The disciple should be warned. At the same time leadership must be sensitive to the direction of the Holy Spirit to "…separate me Barnabas and Saul for the work whereunto I have called them" (Acts 13:2b).

SUMMARY

In Ezekiel's vision of the "Valley of Dry Bones" in Ezekiel 37, we see bones cut off from each other and without life. Ezekiel prophesied over the bones as instructed, and they began to shake and come together. Next, the Lord caused muscle and sinew to form on the bones. As the wind of God filled the bodies, the Word says they: "stood up upon their feet, an exceeding great army."

Many ministers feel this prophecy has fulfillment today in the Body of Christ. God has been shaking believers and churches to come together. He is pouring out His Spirit on all flesh. The end result is an exceeding great army. Not a natural army, but an army of Christlike disciples full of love, who fight a spiritual war against demonic forces and bring healing and blessing to the earth.

> "And so it is written, The first man Adam was made a living soul; the last Adam was made a quickening spirit. Howbeit that was not first which is spiritual, but that which is natural; and afterward that which is spiritual."
>
> —I Corinthians 15:45–46

As with the births of Adam and Christ, prophecy in the Bible often has double fulfillment, first physically and then spiritually. I believe Ezekiel's vision also has double fulfillment, first physically in the nation of Israel and then spiritually in the Body of Christ.

Think of how dry and dead the bones of the Jewish people looked before they became a nation in 1948. For nearly 2000 years the Jewish people were separated from each other.

> "Then he said unto me, Son of man, these bones are the whole house of Israel: behold, they say, Our bones are dried, and our hope is lost: we are cut off for our parts. Therefore prophesy and say unto them, Thus saith the Lord God; Behold, O my people, I will open your graves, and cause you to come up out of your graves, and bring you into the land of Israel."
>
> —Ezekiel 37:11–12

How hopeless it must have looked in the natural for the Lord to bring the Jews back into the land of Israel. They had been separated for millennia. They had assumed different languages and dialects of the nations where they were scattered. They had developed different sects, manner of dress and customs. Yet they were still bound together by the two major things that made them a people: *Circumcision* and the *Passover*. I think of the church, the Body of Christ, divided by our own sects, customs and languages. Yet there remains the same two things that made us a people: The *"circumcision made without hands"* (Col. 2:11) and *"Christ our Passover"* (I Cor. 5:7).

It seems even more unlikely for the Body of Christ to be unified and come to maturity than for the nation of Israel. It took shaking to bring the bones in Ezekiel's vision together. It took a great shaking in the earth to bring about the formation of Israel in 1948. World War II shook the world and Israel was delivered in those birth pains.

> "Again he said unto me, Prophesy upon these bones, and say unto them, O ye dry bones, hear the word of the Lord. Thus saith the Lord God unto these bones; Behold, I will cause breath to enter into you, and ye shall live: And I will lay sinews upon you, and will bring up flesh upon you, and cover you with skin, and put breath in you, and ye shall live; and ye shall know that I am the Lord. So I prophesied as I was commanded: and as I prophesied, there was a noise, and behold a shaking, and the bones came together, bone to his bone."
>
> —Ezekiel 37:4–7

I pray it will not take the natural shakings of war to change the church like it took Israel. My hope is the prophetic Word of the Lord will cause a spiritual shaking.

Humanists have defined the world today as living in a "Post-Christian era." I need not tell you how desperate are the times we live in. We must not continue to do church in the same way. Great changes are needed in the Church if we are to come to Christlike maturity. I pray the truth that I have shared in this manual will help shake church leaders and God's people to change.